The American Management Assc
is a nonprofit educational organizatic
cated to finding, developing, and sharing
better methods of management.

Formed in 1923 by the merger of several
management societies, AMA has as its basic
concern the improvement of management
skills and techniques. The Association does
no lobbying and advances no propaganda.

The AMA program includes courses, conferences, seminars, and research and publication services. This publication is representative of the AMA educational program
—"of management, by management, for
management."

The Marketing
Executive
Of the Future

The Marketing
Executive
Of the Future

By

Patrick J. Montana

American Management Association, Inc.

The Marketing Executive of the Future was originally prepared as a dissertation in partial fulfillment of the requirements for the degree of Doctor of Philosophy for presentation to the faculty of the Graduate School of Business Administration, New York University, during the academic year 1965–1966. The conclusions and opinions expressed herein are those of the author and do not necessarily represent the views of the New York University School of Business Administration, or of individuals, business firms, associates, or agencies contacted.

To the memory of
Dr. Hector Lazo

Preface

Marketing will experience continuing and accelerating change in the years ahead. Change presents challenges, and these will profoundly affect marketing as well as the work and responsibilities of marketing executives. There will be a critical need for more sophisticated and more knowledgeable marketing executives.

Although much has been written about marketing management and the new marketing concept, little has been written about marketing personnel. Are marketing managers receiving the training required to cope effectively with the challenges ahead, or are there inadequacies in development programs as presently constituted? And what improvement, if any, should be made in those programs?

This book identifies the challenges and executive marketing personnel needs of the future, scrutinizes current marketing executive development programs and practices—revealed through a study of selected corporations, colleges and universities, and professional associations—and recommends changes that should be made to improve the development and training of marketing executives so that they will be better able to meet these challenges and needs. It reflects the results of a survey conducted by the author in 1964 and updated in 1966–1967. Current marketing executive development programs and practices of 70 firms listed in the *Fortune* directory of the 500 largest U.S. corporations and of leading universities and professional associations furnished the data for this study.

Acknowledgments

I wish to express my great indebtedness to those company representatives who gave generously of their time when interviewed and to the many others, individuals and organizations, who participated in the study on which this book is based.

A special word of gratitude is due my wife Rosina for her patience and assistance. Her typing skills, editorial advice, and enthusiastic encouragement were invaluable.

Contents

The Marketing
Executive
Of the Future

Introduction

The marketing executive is the new key figure in industry. So states an article in *News Front* magazine.[1] His current rise in the corporate hierarchy has paralleled the dramatic and comparatively recent rise of the marketing concept in the thinking of top management.

The *News Front* article emphasized the importance of finding and training the right people for the marketing team. It stated: "You must develop marketing manpower who can and will carry the marketing program to a successful and profitable conclusion."[2]

In September 1962 a group of top marketing executives discussed this need at a National Industrial Conference Board session in New York City. One of the participants, Harold C. Buell, vice president of P.R. Mallory Company, surveyed approximately 600 companies in various segments of industry.

[1] "The Marketing Executive: Industry's New Crown Prince," *News Front*, August 1963, p. 33.
[2] *Ibid.*

The response: 30 percent replied. The result: Fewer than half of those companies have a planned marketing training program. Among those with programs, about 63 percent rate their efforts as fair at best; some call their own programs poor. Buell concluded: "Most companies are aware of the need for a marketing training program, but they are not doing much about it."

Another participant commented: "We have no formal program for training inside marketing staff—it's mostly by osmosis. I feel this deters good young men from joining our company."

"Developing the future marketing leaders becomes increasingly important under today's competitive marketing conditions," reported C. S. Gischel, vice president–marketing of The Stanley Works.[3]

Rapidly evolving marketing processes and a continually changing environment point to the critical need for well-trained marketing executives. Current trends show that the practitioners of the function of marketing will be expected to carry an even greater share of the responsibility of business in the future. The development of marketing executives who can improve the effectiveness of marketing and meet the challenges of tomorrow has become more important than at any other time in history.

The marketing executive of the future will have key responsibility in the creation and delivery of a standard of living—in bringing to reality the concept of marketing.

Marketing has been explained and interpreted in many different ways. In the past, it has been variously defined in terms of commodities (the commodity approach), institutions (the institutional approach), or functions (the functional approach). These definitions and others which have been formulated hardly convey the customer-oriented concept of current marketing.

The customer-oriented viewpoint is described by Charles F. St. Thomas as ". . . a way of managing a business so that each critical decision is made with a full and prior knowledge of the

[3] "Top Flight Marketing Needed," *Iron Age*, September 27, 1962, p. 51.

impact of that decision on the customer." [4] Peter F. Drucker further amplifies this view of marketing: ". . . Marketing is . . . the whole business seen from the point of view of the final result, that is, from the customer's point of view. Concern and responsibility for marketing must therefore permeate all areas of the enterprise." [5]

Customer-orientation is the very essence of the marketing concept. Lazo and Corbin define this concept as:

> The orientation of all marketing functions toward the customer, and the making of all management decisions in the light of customer needs and for the purpose of satisfying those needs at minimum expense, with optimum sales volume and profit.[6]

The significance of this concept in terms of developing marketing executives was emphasized by Buell when he said:

> Much has been written in the last few years about the marketing concept and why it is necessary to business profit and survival. More and more companies have assigned a marketing title to a top executive and are expecting him to define markets and establish plans for reaching them. But while they are thinking about improved marketing concepts, most companies seem to do little to train the staffs assigned to put marketing policies into practice. In fact, we wonder if many of today's marketing staffs are not actually sales departments with a different title. We wonder how many companies are still following the old practice of manufacturing a product and then telling the sales department to go out and sell it with the help of the marketing department.

> In recent years industry has shown an active interest in long-range planning. Elaborate programs have been developed to analyze products, facilities, research and finance and coordinate them into a master plan. Obviously, marketing oc-

[4] "A Basic Guide to Marketing for the Smaller Company," *Industrial Marketing*, June 1959, p. 4.

[5] *The Practice of Management*, Harper & Row, New York, pp. 38–39.

[6] Lazo, Hector, and Arnold Corbin, *Management in Marketing*, McGraw-Hill Book Company, New York, 1961, p. 74.

cupies a major place in these long term plans and forecasts. However, if marketing is to perform its required function, we must think seriously about training our marketing staffs in more sophisticated marketing techniques. It's no longer adequate for them to be indoctrinated with company and product philosophy.

It's popular these days to say that marketing must have top management approval and support. However, if top management is to lean more heavily on the marketing function, it must have assurance that the marketing staff is thoroughly competent to analyze, make recommendations and implement a marketing program. Effective marketing can only result from staffs of qualified marketing people and they will only be qualified if they are well trained.[7]

In this book, questions of key importance to the marketing executive of the future will be explored in depth. These will include:

1. What emerging trends present challenges to the marketing executive of the future?

2. What skills and knowledge do these trends and changes demand that the effective marketing executive acquire?

3. Given the necessity of acquiring these skills and knowledge, what personal action can practicing or aspiring marketing executives take to equip themselves properly?

4. To what extent are companies assisting current or aspiring marketing executives to equip themselves? To what extent should companies do this? Should the burden be placed primarily on personal action or on formal company action?

5. To what extent are colleges and universities and professional associations providing marketing education for current or aspiring executives? Are these programs geared to dovetail more with personal action or company action?

6. What are the guidelines for the future?

[7] Speech by Harold C. Buell, vice president of P. R. Mallory Company, at the 10th Annual Marketing Conference, New York, National Industrial Conference Board, September 29, 1962.

Part One

MARKETING MANAGEMENT IN TOMORROW'S WORLD

1

The Challenges Ahead

The marketing challenges of the future have been predicted by many of today's leading authorities and business experts. A typical opinion is expressed by Herbert D. Bissell, vice president–marketing at Honeywell, Incorporated:

> The marketing function is becoming so significant in American business life today that a good marketing man should be involved in many of the significant decisions made by a corporation. I think marketing is going to become increasingly poignant, more scientific, more computer oriented and generally more vital to the profit success of any enterprise.[1]

From a careful reading of this forecast and others like it, the marketing executive of the future can identify emerging trends and their implications.

[1] See Buell, Victor P., *Marketing Management in Action*, McGraw-Hill Book Company, New York, 1966, p. 284.

THE INCREASED TEMPO OF CHANGE

The touchstone of tomorrow's market will be change. That change has always been with us is an obvious fact of life which managers must face. The current significance of change, however, is that managers are accepting it as a normal condition of business life and are also accepting the fact that the rate and pace of change are accelerating rapidly.[2]

In describing the management challenges that lie ahead, Richard Allen Stull [3] points to four significant factors:

  1. Many new products and materials.
  2. Fast changes in distribution channels.
  3. Higher selling cost and greater profit challenge.
  4. Increased competition at home and abroad.

He explains:

> It will be difficult for most companies to be in the running without a market-oriented approach to management decisions. . . . "Brand loyalty" will no longer be a safe bet. . . . The marketing-for-profit approach will dominate management thinking. Company plans will be predicated on buyers' needs. The profit rather than volume approach to selling will be almost universal.[4]

Stull goes on to predict a dramatic role for the marketing executive of the future:

> Marketing managers will not only participate in production and finance but, in many companies, will be the strongest voices in planning. The top marketing man will often be a staff man who will coordinate field sales, advertising, merchandising, promotion, public relations and marketing research.[5]

[2] See Healy, James H., "Six Challenges for Tomorrow's Manager," *Dun's Review and Modern Industry*, October 1964, p. 32.
[3] "Management Challenges for the 1970's," *Advanced Management Journal*, January 1965, p. 45.
[4] *Ibid.*
[5] *Ibid.*

SHIFTS IN MANPOWER

Population growth and the distribution of age groups will significantly affect the marketing world of tomorrow. By 1970, the population of the United States will reach an estimated 210 million. The percentage of the population over the age of 65 is rising and will continue to rise because of a lengthening of the life span. Eric W. Vetter [6] points out that as business needs for capable managers expand, a relatively small percentage of our population will be between the ages of 30 and 45—the age group that plays the most significant role in middle management and professional jobs. The U.S. Department of Labor estimates that this group will constitute only 11 percent of the population in 1970 and will drop to 10 percent by 1975. These projections must have a significant impact on long-range manpower planning for the next decade.

ACCELERATED GROWTH OF AUTOMATION

The trend toward automation is apparent today, and its continued and accelerated growth will greatly alter the market of the future. George C. Houston [7] notes the impact of this trend toward automation in the coupling of mounting investment in plant and equipment with greater risk and heavier penalties for inadequate planning and organizing. The greater the rate of automation, the more intense is the need for retraining and development of higher skills and specialized know-how.

Administrative automation has only scratched the surface of the executive's need for a wider variety of usable information faster than ever before, states Don G. Mitchell.[8] A feature re-

[6] "The Nature of Long-Range Manpower Planning," *Management of Personnel Quarterly*, Summer 1964, pp. 23–24.

[7] *Manager Development—Principles and Perspectives*, Richard D. Irwin, Inc., Homewood, Ill., 1961, p. 81.

[8] *The Challenges Facing Management*, New York University Press, 1963, p. 9.

port in *Business Week* points out the impact of automation in these terms: "The computer is flashing with dazzling speed across the panorama of marketing—which takes in the entire relationship between the designer of a product, the manufacturer, seller, buyer and user." [9] The ability to respond to the challenge of automation is essential to the marketing executive of the future.

IMPROVED MANAGERIAL TECHNIQUES

The next decade will see increasing use of new quantitative methods, such as operations research, data processing, statistical analysis, and the critical path method in the analysis and planning of business operations. An article in *Nation's Business* indicates that "significant advances are now being made in a basic understanding of information of all kinds and the manner in which it is interwoven in business decision-making." [10] Houston [11] highlights the significance of this trend when he says that improved abilities to assemble, analyze, and use more and better information in planning, organizing, operation, and control of the total enterprise will permit managers to take greater risks with confidence.

WORLDWIDE BUSINESS OPERATIONS

The trend toward increased international business activity is already discernible in today's market. According to Mitchell, former president of General Telephone and Electronic Corporation: "The challenge is to establish manufacturing and service facilities abroad in order to participate in the expansion of markets there." [12] He further states that Western Europe

[9] "Computers begin to solve the marketing puzzle," April 17, 1965, p. 118.
[10] "Businessman of the Future," January 1964, p. 25.
[11] *Op. cit.*, pp. 81–82.
[12] *Op. cit.*, p. 12.

presents American industry with its greatest opportunity and its greatest challenge and estimates that sales from overseas operations will at least double in the next ten years.

Before a meeting of the Sales Executives Club of New York in 1964, Fred J. Borch, president and chief executive officer of the General Electric Company, forecast a growing internationalization of industry and its customers—with a rise of more international corporations, worldwide markets, and intensified competition. "American enterprise," he explained, "has entered a new era of worldwide economic relationships of significance to every family in the land."

INTERDEPENDENCE OF GOVERNMENT AND BUSINESS

Evident to all forecasters of the market of the future is the increasing trend toward business-government relations. This development will bring mixed blessings to the world of marketing. Government activities are opening new markets in such areas as educational systems and automated highways. Governmental power is expected to substantially increase enforcement of social and economic policies in such areas as racial integration and air and water pollution.

A feature report in *Nation's Business* cites the growing dependence of substantial elements of the American business community on governmental programs. The article explores the possibility of "increased cooperation between private industry and government . . . as the cold war spreads into bitter economic warfare between East and West, and as powerful new economic blocs emerge as competitive threats." [13]

IMPROVED TECHNOLOGIES

Increasing technological advances from scientific and industrial research will complicate the decision-making process in the

[13] "Businessman of the Future," *op. cit.*, p. 24.

decades ahead. Expenditures in this area will at least double over the next few years. There will be a marked jump in the rate of technological obsolescence as well as an increasing competition of ideas. Both Houston and Mitchell imply that the marketing position of the United States in the next decade will depend on the skill and speed with which we shorten the time lag between discovery and use of new knowledge and ideas.

NEW FORMS OF COMPETITION

New forms of competition are emerging that will set the pace and direction of the market in the years ahead. Houston states the challenge this way:

> Fewer companies will be competing for the same markets. There will be competition between technologies as well as competition between different products serving the same need. Increased foreign competition in the domestic market and increased competition for share of world markets will add up to new and changing markets.[14]

The identification of these emerging trends clearly indicates the challenge of the market of the future. And that challenge is *change*. The marketing executive of the future cannot ignore that challenge. To meet it, he will need to acquire new skills and knowledge.

[14] *Op. cit.,* p. 82.

2

New Dimensions of the Marketing Manager's Job

The trends and changes which will characterize tomorrow's market demand that the effective marketing executive acquire certain skills and knowledge.

MANAGING INNOVATION AND CHANGE

The marketing manager of tomorrow must be creative, flexible, curious, imaginative, and a master of the daring art of innovation. The challenge of the market of the next decade requires him to become more and more the manager of change. To accomplish this, the marketing manager must develop a

27

policy of constant vigilance—keeping continually abreast of new knowledge and changes affecting his business, sifting the relevant from the irrelevant, and interpreting and applying this knowledge. He must understand and implement the philosophy, theory, and process of managing, planning, and strategy; of organizing; of authority, delegation, and cooperative action; and of measuring the performance of the business and of individuals in the business.

Educating and Developing Managers

Tomorrow's marketing executive must spend more time on manager education and development. His challenge will be to encourage and to direct individual self-development. The successful fulfillment of this basic responsibility will insure the progress and survival of his individual business.

Increasing population growth and shifts in the distribution of age groups will present signal difficulties in the education and development of future managers. But there is no particular magic involved in this process. The marketing executive has only to acquire systematically knowledge of the teaching-learning process and its essential skills; personnel selection and placement; manager-manpower planning; individual performance appraisal; and planning and implementation of self-development.

Understanding the Computer

Increasingly, the manager in marketing must learn to think in terms of computer applications, of systems, of processes, and of relationships. He must develop a real understanding of the computer and of its role in the decision-making process. The language of the computer must become as familiar to him as his own—for, in the next decade, it is not unreasonable to expect computers to be making a variety of decisions that middle and top executives now spend time making. Understanding the use of the computer in developing information systems that consist of more than financial data also is essential. To effectively harness the computer's power to marketing's chariot, the marketing executive must grasp the concept of the business as an integrated system—encompassing the functional contributions of the individual and the team in achieving the common objectives of the business.

LONG-RANGE DECISION MAKING

In the next decade, the manager in marketing will make decisions of longer-range impact. The Monday morning quarterback will suffer heavier risks and penalties for poor judgment; many decisions will be irreversible. His thorough understanding of the technological, economic, social, and political forces in the business environment as well as of the objectives, markets, and material, financial, and human resources of the individual business will be essential to the decision-making process.

APPLYING NEW MANAGEMENT CONCEPTS

The marketing executive will be required to become an environmentalist—taking an active part in shaping his environment and the future of his business in it. He must be aware of the increasing fund of knowledge, experience, and research findings in economics and the social sciences. These powerful tools can help him create conditions which foster business growth and progress. But the marketing manager must know how to employ these tools—to utilize what he has learned about human needs and motivations—in relation to employees, customers, and others with whom he has direct contact as well as with the public at large.

In addition, the manager of marketing must learn well the implications of the increasing trend toward international business activity. He must understand the philosophies, cultures, and politics of other peoples and nations as well as he does those of the United States. The reason for this is clear: "The day of the multinational corporation is already here, and the day when a substantial portion of American production will be either manufactured or sold abroad is not far off." [1]

Briefly, then, the marketing executive of the future must be prepared to become a member of a new corps of international citizens—managers with a strong background in the psychology and techniques of the effective communication of ideas as well as in the theory and process of social cooperation.

COLLABORATING WITH THE GOVERNMENT

The next decade will see greater interaction between political science and business, and the manager of marketing will become increasingly concerned with business-government relations. Congressional decisions and attitudes, for example, will have greater weight in his decision making. To take an obvious example:

> One cannot study marketing problems in the defense industry . . . without also understanding how military budgets and procurement programs are put together on the government's side and how Congressional attitudes toward the defense budget are determined.[2]

---

[1] "Businessman of the Future," *Nation's Business,* January 1964, p. 39.
[2] Cyert, Richard M., and William R. Dill, "The Future of Business Education," *The Journal of Business,* July 1964, p. 230.

ANTICIPATING SCIENTIFIC AND TECHNOLOGICAL ADVANCES

The marketing executive must learn to anticipate new scientific and technological advances. Before new ideas are developed into realities, he must be prepared to cope with their implications for his business. New products will flood the marketplace, fresh ideas will appear at every turn in the road. The marketing executive, therefore, must place increasing emphasis on setting long-range goals and on establishing systematic programs for achieving them as essential means of determining where a company should go and how it should get there.

BECOMING CUSTOMER-ORIENTED

The manager of marketing must become more and more market- or customer-oriented, gaining a sound yardstick to measure changing customer needs, wants, attitudes, and buying habits as well as to measure the effects of such factors as performance, reliability, quality, price, and customer service on the value of products or services. He must quickly recognize opportunities for the improvement of existing products and services or for the development of new ones. He must have a keen understanding of exactly who his customer is or could be.

ACQUIRING FLEXIBILITY

Finally, to practice successfully the art and science of marketing in tomorrow's business world, the marketing executive must learn to enjoy the stimulation of a constantly changing and expanding environment. He must recognize the fact that both position requirements and organizational structure will continue to change. And he must welcome these changes, for he will be armed with the necessary skills and knowledge that will make him a manager equal to the challenges of tomorrow, not the challenges of yesterday.

Part Two

DEVELOPING TOMORROW'S MARKETING EXECUTIVES

3

Personal Action

The men who manage American business agree that "today's recruit for a marketing job should be a literate man, who will continue to learn after he has left the campus. . . ."[1] Says Owen R. Slauson, vice president-marketing for Ray-O-Vac Company: ". . . Knowledge, whether from formal education or private study and/or experience, is essential."[2] The practicing or potential marketing executive is fortunate in being able to engage in a wide variety of activities to acquire and develop the skills and knowledge needed to manage effectively in the years ahead.

FOLLOWING A READING PROGRAM

One of the ways in which the marketing executive may acquire the knowledge that will be necessary is to pursue a con-

[1] "Getting More Out of the Graduate," *Business Week*, June 18, 1966, p. 64.
[2] Buell, Victor, P., *Marketing Management in Action*, McGraw-Hill Book Company, New York, 1966, p. 284.

tinuing program of reading in the field of marketing. He should first read a current textbook on the principles of marketing to gain a perspective and background in the field. He should regularly read such publications as the *Harvard Business Review, Fortune, Journal of Marketing, Dun's Review,* and *Sales Management.* In addition, the marketing executive should cultivate the habit of reading at least one book a month in the area of marketing. He might, for example, list the various functional areas of marketing and select the most current book in the area in which he feels the highest interest. He should attempt to spread his reading throughout the entire discipline of the marketing field.

Interested groups of marketing executives from the same company or from different companies might get together on a regular basis to discuss a selected book. In this way, the individual marketing specialist will be able to keep abreast of the latest writings in each of the functional areas of marketing. At the same time, he will be able to sharpen his thinking in the field and broaden his outlook on marketing by sharing views with other interested marketing executives.

Building a Ready-Reference File

To keep his thinking up to date, the marketing executive should also keep an index card file on marketing information that he thinks will be useful in the future. For example, as he hears or reads about new trends, knowledge, tools, and applications in the field of marketing, he might summarize the information and write the name of a source to which he can refer for additional data on an index card. In this way he will build a ready-reference file on marketing information for current and future use.

JOINING A PROFESSIONAL ASSOCIATION

Another step that the marketing executive can take personally to equip himself properly is to participate actively in at least one professional association in the field of marketing. He might choose the American Marketing Association, the Sales Executives Club, or any of the many other industrial or trade organizations that meet the needs of the executive. Taking an active part in the local chapter activities of these associations offers many advantages to the marketing manager. Chief among these is the opportunity to acquire skills and knowledge that will assist him in meeting the challenges of the future.

PUBLISHING AND LECTURING

One of the more rewarding personal activities which the actual or aspiring marketing executive can undertake to equip himself properly with the new skills and knowledge necessary in the years ahead is to contribute to the profession through publications and lectures. The preparation of well-thought-out articles and lectures forces the executive to learn more through research and study. At the same time, it serves to build his reputation in the field.

Whenever possible, it is highly beneficial for the marketing manager to teach a course in marketing at a nearby college or junior college. Experience with students in the classroom will aid him in developing marketing know-how in his own business.

UPGRADING SKILLS THROUGH TRAINING

The marketing executive can equip himself with new skills and knowledge through additional training in company and noncompany programs and through formal education. Courses and seminars offered by colleges and universities, professional and trade associations, corporations, and various governmental and volunteer groups can be of great value in equipping the marketing executive to successfully meet the challenges of the future.

Honeywell's Herbert D. Bissell makes the point that in certain organizations it takes an unusually enlightened central management to recognize the division man with exceptional talents and provide him with "a variety of experiences that broaden his horizons and prepare him for general management as he matures." [3] And a study on management development indicates that—

> . . . The usual approach to part-time training involves encouragement and occasional guidance in the selection of programs but very little direction and nomination of individuals for training. . . . The decision to apply for these offerings usually is made by the individual manager, although his superior may guide him in this decision.[4]

Acquiring the knowledge and skills needed to tackle the marketing management jobs of the future obviously is too important a task to leave to chance. Self-motivation is an essential ingredient in achieving executive success. Lee S. Bickmore, president of National Biscuit Company, makes this clear when he says: "Many people would like to be successful . . . but few are willing to make the sacrifices necessary. They won't prepare for it; they won't qualify themselves. . . ." [5]

Essentially, the practicing or aspiring marketing executive must be eager to acquire any new knowledge, tool, or skill which has any application to his chosen profession. His ability to remain receptive to new ideas and his creativity in applying

[3] *Ibid.,* p. 288.

[4] Mahoney, Thomas A., *Building the Executive Team: A Guide to Management Development,* Prentice-Hall, Inc., Englewood, New Jersey, 1961, p. 243.

[5] "Success Has Four Price Tags," *Reader's Digest,* March 1965, p. 69.

new knowledge will become his most important skills. Leadership, drive, administrative skills, the ability to make decisions, and empathy with people at all levels are listed by one marketing management study [6] as desirable characteristics of the marketing manager of the future. Considered essential also is experience in—or exposure to—such areas as sales, advertising, production, research and development, and accounting. But, above all, the future marketing leader's success will depend to a high degree upon his capacity to grow.

[6] See Buell, V. P., *op. cit.*, pp. 285–286.

4

Company Programs
and Policies

The survey of company programs and practices conducted by the author sheds considerable light on the extent to which companies assist the practicing or aspiring marketing executive to equip himself with needed skills and knowledge. Certain underlying patterns clearly emerge.[1]

PROGRAM AIMS AND PHILOSOPHIES

Few major corporations recognize the critical need for a formal marketing executive development program. Fully 50 percent of the 40 firms responding reported no formal program at all, with another 7.5 percent reporting such programs now on the drawing board. The majority of the 42.5 percent reporting

[1] Detailed observations of data collected during guided personal interviews with representatives of 40 companies precedes general observations of data collected from all 70 corporations included in the survey.

40

formal programs actually offer little more than a sales training program aimed primarily at developing salesmen or a general management development program designed primarily to prepare and aid most managers in the company in their present and future jobs. In addition, the majority of companies offering a formal marketing program make it available to new employees only. All but a handful overlook the value of giving old company employees an equal opportunity to acquire new skills and knowledge.

Since most of the formal programs have been in existence for only a short time—five years or less, approximately—it appears that increasing importance is now attached by American industry to developing marketing executives of the future. This pattern is strengthened by the intended development of such programs in firms which previously had no such effort.

The programs of a majority of the companies surveyed are aimed at developing an adequate supply of well-prepared managers for future marketing and management positions. Few, however, possess clear-cut and specific aims or objectives. Underlying many stated aims is a basic recognition that big business can no longer depend solely upon the evolutionary growth of executives—one of the most critical problems currently facing top management. This need is especially evident in marketing, where, according to Lazo and Corbin, "the marketing concept has highlighted the need for qualified marketing executives in a field which has received less attention in the thinking of top management than many other fields of management." [2]

A significant weakness is the lack of any statement of philosophy of marketing executive development. This may be interpreted to mean either that many companies have a philosophy that is not in writing or that they operate without any guiding principle at all in the development of marketing executives.

A recognition of the importance of customer orientation is

[2] Lazo, Hector, and Arnold Corbin, *Management in Marketing*, McGraw-Hill Book Co., New York, 1961, p. 470.

evident in the philosophy stated by several firms. This emphasizes the need for developing marketing executives who will
implement this philosophy in the years ahead. Generally, too,
there is division within a company between the responsibility
for a development program and its implementation. Top management most frequently has primary responsibility for marketing executive development. But while top management oversees
the program, the bulk of the actual development work must be
done through the heads of the operating units of the company.

Programs vary considerably from company to company. The
following descriptions indicate how four corporations are assisting in the development of marketing executives.

PERSONNEL DEVELOPMENT: COMPANY *A*

The overall personnel development plans in the many marketing components of Company *A,* with its approximately
275,000 employees, are formalized into a general marketing
manpower plan. This manpower plan is then analyzed together
with the overall marketing plan for the business, and the findings are reflected in terms of the personnel development areas
of work. These findings can be grouped as follows:

1. Forecast of manpower needs—short and long range—as
to both number of men and knowledge and skills required.
2. Inventory of current personnel.
3. Recruiting, selection, and placement of personnel.
4. Training needs and plans for all employees.
5. Employee compensation plans.
6. Provisions for an individual development plan for each
employee.

However, the decisive area of manpower development in a marketing component lies, first of all, in the conscious effort of the
manager of marketing to establish a climate, a working atmo-
sphere, in which every person in the organization is stimulated,

encouraged, and guided to develop his own powers to his maximum potential.

In this company, a new approach is reflected in current marketing executive development activity. It is based upon a change in management philosophy and practice that has resulted from adoption of significantly different basic assumptions about human behavior. The concepts suggested are the product of serious thought by leaders in the field of management and are based upon the accumulated knowledge of human behavior contributed by many specialized sciences.

These concepts are fundamental to the creation of a climate conducive to maximum self-development. Thus, in Company *A*, the key to more effective appraisal and development lies in the manager's view of his subordinates and his relationship with them rather than in the form and routine of the process itself. Most successful managers can recall one or more outstanding "developers of men" with whom they have worked and to whom they give credit for much of their personal progress. Many such managers recall a period when elaborate procedures and forms did not exist, yet the inspiration given them lasted throughout their careers.

In such a company, self-development planning is the responsibility of each individual. Managers can guide the employee in the preparation of prescriptive and demanding individual plans; can encourage and facilitate the carrying out of these plans; can set high performance standards; and can periodically appraise performance against those standards and review the individual's progress on his development program.

The development process in this company follows a logical chronology:

1. Preparation of work plans for the immediate period ahead and the establishment of standards of performance.
2. Appraisal of work performance against these standards.
3. Appraisal of the individual's demonstrated capabilities and his growth potential.

4. Preparation of the self-development plan.

The process described ties the overall business plan to the marketing plans for the business and to a formal marketing manpower plan. It sets the stage for intelligent planning for growth in terms of marketing executive development.

With a knowledge of the business goals it seeks to attain, tied to a knowledge of the marketing manpower needed to achieve these goals, the company can plan much more effectively by determining the talent it already has and the talent it needs to reach its goals, and finally by deciding what must be done to provide the talent and skills that will be necessary.

The outstanding feature of the program is the importance of the managerial influence on development. This influence, together with the self-development planning approach—which is based on certain work plans and measurable standards of performance for each employee—makes this one of the more extensive and elaborate programs in terms of marketing executive development.

The training program is strictly marketing personnel-oriented rather than sales or general management-oriented in that it draws its marketing manpower from any of seven marketing components: sales, advertising and sales promotion, marketing research, product planning, marketing administration, product service, and marketing personnel development. The experience gained by marketing executives under the company's development approach in these various marketing functions provides them with the necessary training for future high-level marketing managerial positions.

Personnel Development: Company *B*

The concept of development planning in this company, whose employees number approximately 30,000, is directed toward preparing qualified individuals for future responsibilities and assuring a reservoir of qualified persons for movement into future position openings of the company.[3]

Divisional marketing managers are responsible for identifying long-range organization and manpower needs and for development planning to meet these needs. More than one individual might be prepared for any one future position. Development of an individual for another position can be accelerated through the planning of experiences to provide opportunity for acquiring needed knowledge and skills, and by creating an awareness on the part of the individual that development opportunities exist.

Development planning is composed of four elements:

1. Position requirements of a specific future position.
2. Individual requirements of the ideal candidate.
3. Individual qualifications of a specific candidate.
4. Planned experiences for a specific individual.

The planned experiences for any individual must be directed toward a specific future position in order to give purpose to those experiences. The particular experiences on the job or off the job should fit a particular individual and his particular needs. Development, or growth, of the individual is a result of the planned experiences; it is not the means.

The divisional marketing manager has primary responsibility for development planning for the individual in preparation for future responsibility. He is the key person in identifying individuals most likely to advance, making necessary arrangements, and obtaining approval for an individual to have needed planned experiences on the job or off the job. The individual may or may not know the purpose of the planned experiences.

The whole process is a continuous one and is related to the timing of long-range organization needs and "estimate of readiness" reports for marketing executives.

---

[3] See Chapter 5 for an in-depth description of a product manager's job under this concept.

Apparently, significant progress has been made through this program in the following ways:

1. Better understanding of the job expectations between individual and superior.

2. More thorough review of the qualifications of an individual in terms of what is needed for a job.

3. Better establishment of objectives by which an individual can be measured, these being established by the individuals, not handed down necessarily by management.

4. Better planning to accomplish these stated objectives.

5. Greater emphasis on identifying the improvement needs for an individual, rather than a punitive evaluation of his performance.

Since 1962, the company has been providing more internal development opportunities as opposed to sending executives to outside professional association programs. Examples of this activity are a product management training program, sponsored by the corporate marketing staff; a division marketing program, currently being developed for international marketing personnel; and some skill-type training, sponsored by the corporate personnel staff.

PERSONNEL DEVELOPMENT: COMPANY *C*

The philosophy of this company, with about 25,000 employees, is that it should be training executives, not solely for its marketing operation, but rather for the company as a whole. The primary purposes of its program are not only constant improvement of executives in their present positions but also the development of these employees to meet future company needs. Its stated methods for developing employees consist of the following:

1. Closely examine the existing personnel and determine, as best as possible, the potential of each man.

2. Continually review future organizational needs against existing personnel.

3. Assist each individual to improve his performance on his present assignment.

4. Assist individuals who have potential for further advancement to broaden themselves, through job rotation and through formal and informal training, so as to prepare themselves to meet organization needs.

The development program covers all administrative, supervisory, and professional employees. It often takes in many other employees who, in the opinion of their supervisors, have potential for management.

Each year, vice presidents, plant managers, other principal department heads, and other management people throughout the company evaluate all the men reporting directly to them through discussion with a representative of the personnel administration department. The following factors are discussed concerning each person:

1. Educational background and previous work experience.

2. All aspects of present performance.

3. Strengths.

4. Any significant weaknesses.

5. Potential.

6. An individual development plan for the coming year.

7. Follow-ups or backstops throughout the company for each position.

The supervisor and the personnel representative discuss at length the broadening of individuals for better performance on their present jobs and for greater future responsibilities. Definite plans are then made on a plantwide and companywide basis for rotation of employees with high potential to assignments both inside and outside the scope of their present departments. All the individual evaluations are then reviewed by the top executives of the company.

This same policy is followed in developing executives for

47

the marketing division. For example, when a new marketing trainee first enters the company, he spends several weeks having discussions with representatives from the various departments in the company so that he can learn more about them and their functions in the company. During this time, he visits every department, including plant operations. He is then sent out to the field sales organization for a period of about 14 months. This amount of time is necessary because the company prefers to have him gain practical sales experience in its several product divisions. Throughout this period, some time is also spent by the trainee in formalized sales training programs. In addition, the company prefers to have him gain supervisory experience in each of its several product divisions.

Following completion of his assignment in the field sales organization, the trainee is transferred back to the marketing department and assigned to each of the separate operations in the company, such as the general promotion department, the market research department, the advertising department, and each of the product marketing groups. This gives the company an opportunity to assess the interests and talents of the individual in each of these various areas and also gives the individual concerned an opportunity to determine for himself which area of the business appeals most to him. The company tries to determine as early as possible where the trainee would be best suited and then assigns him to that area for a period of about one year to gain basic background experience in marketing. Keeping in mind the interests and aspirations of the trainee, the company then tries to transfer the man to some of the other areas of the business for additional background training.

A significant feature of the program is that it provides the future marketing manager with the experience he will require to manage in a customer-oriented company. The sales and supervisory experience gained in the various product divisions enables the future marketing executive to learn substantially about the products and the customers of the company. During this phase of his marketing training, the salesman spends some time in educating his customers in the marketing aspects of the product. At the same time, he learns the customers' needs and wants. His return to the marketing department—plus the on-the-job training he then receives in the various marketing functions in each of the product marketing groups—serves to continue his marketing education in the company.

At the completion of this training, a man has the background experience and knowledge necessary to qualify him for future marketing managerial positions. The program has worked very well to date in providing trained marketing management personnel.

PERSONNEL DEVELOPMENT: COMPANY *D*

There are two formal training programs in this company with about 7,000 employees—a product management program and a sales management program.

The product management program is designed to give the college graduate or the qualified employee broad practical experience in advertising, sales, and merchandising. The program has been carefully worked out over the years to help trainees develop sufficient marketing skills for responsible leadership.

The training program starts with a one-week orientation period in the New York office and covers company background, policies, and products. The subsequent six months are spent learning the field sales job and acquiring first-hand knowledge of sales, advertising, and merchandising as applied to small retail stores and large retail chains.

Men who show potential and interest in advertising and merchandising continue their product management program at the home office in New York. This means the next year is spent in on-the-job assignments in the sales promotion department, the market research department, and an international advertising agency. Each assignment lasts three months. This phase of training provides practical experience in the advertising and merchandising skills needed for the creation and execution of sales promotion and national advertising campaigns. Throughout this period trainees work closely with experienced specialists and are given the opportunity to make productive contributions to the projects assigned to them. As stated in the recruiting literature of the company, these job experiences, plus seminars in advertising and merchandising, offer thorough preparation for advancement.

Upon the satisfactory conclusion of this initial training, it is possible for men showing potential and interest in sales to change to the sales management training program. In this case, the man is assigned a permanent sales territory as a division salesman. Growth may continue in field sales, as assistant division manager, and then as division manager. It is possible to transfer to the planning and development of overall sales objectives in the home office, as well as to positions in product management, sales promotion, and market research.

At the end of this basic training, a man is promoted to product manager assistant with a product group. Advancement continues as rapidly as the man is ready for more responsibility—to assistant product manager and then to product manager. A man will generally spend six months in each of the "assistant" positions before he becomes a product manager.

Every effort is made to develop men to their full potential and promote them to appropriate positions as quickly as practical business procedure allows. In addition to promotion, transfers are made from one product group to another to provide broad experience in all the company's products. This provides invaluable training for eventual promotion to top marketing management.

Because of the international scope of the business, it is also possible for product managers to be transferred to major over-seas offices for a few years to broaden their experience further. Then they usually return to the home office in New York to be assigned either to the international or to the domestic operation.

The program seems to have worked well for the company over the years in providing executives qualified to fill top marketing managerial positions. The product management program, which has been in existence for many years, provides on-the-job experience in the marketing functions among the various product groups to qualify the candidates for future high-level marketing positions. The effectiveness of the training program in accomplishing its objectives is exemplified by the fact that more than 50 percent of the executives on the current top overall management organization chart are products of these programs.

OVERALL EVALUATION

The corporations surveyed stress on-the-job training as the most effective marketing executive development procedure. Over 50 percent favor developing marketing executives through *doing* activities (on-the-job training) rather than *thinking* activities (generally off-the-job training). Thus present practices for developing marketing executives do not differ from past practices.

In general, development programs are centrally coordinated. Central coordination of the marketing executive development program attaches a degree of importance to this activity in an organization.

Corporation managements for the most part believe that they have a systematic and orderly method for determining their present and future marketing managerial needs. Those who do not have such a method feel that they know their manpower needs well and that through their policy of promotion from within competent personnel will filter to the top to fill their managerial requirements.

In recent years, more exposure to the competition, more reliance on formal instruction, more effort in product management, and greater familiarity with other functions have changed the emphasis placed on different procedures for marketing executive development. In some instances, the changed procedures or the change in emphasis has been slight. In others, the changes are too new to evaluate. Companies are still groping in this area.

When companies evaluate their own programs, they usually employ informal evaluation procedures that lack clearly defined objectives. At best, evaluation methods are subjective and are not based upon any stated or written objectives. The following quotations illustrate the methods used by several corporations to evaluate their programs:

- "Statistical analysis, control groups, and interviews."
- "Turnover figures and availability of people for promotion."
- "Through the candidates and by means of a questionnaire."
- "By departments and the training division, penetration of market, increasing volume, and acceptance of new products."
- "Feedback procedure on a day-to-day basis."

Exhibit 1 shows how corporations rate their own programs. Although these companies willingly rate their programs, the soundness of their basis for ratings may be questioned in the light of the substantial number of firms that admit a lack of objectives for evaluation. Most companies rate their own programs neither good nor excellent.

The importance of determining marketing executive needs is evidenced by the fact that middle- to top-level management is involved in this activity in a substantial number of corpora-

EXHIBIT 1

How Companies Rate Their Own Programs

[Self-rating of marketing executive development
programs by respondents from 40 selected large
U.S. corporations]

Rating	No. of Companies	% of Companies
Poor	4	10
Fair	8	20
Fair to good	10	25
Good	8	20
Excellent	6	15
No response	4	10
Total	40	100

tions. Exhibit 2 lists the titles of the persons responsible for determining marketing executive needs.

On the average, five years is a reasonable target for a company to aim at in projecting marketing executive needs. Five years gives a company ample time to provide the programs necessary to recruit, select, place, and develop the marketing executives who will manage the business in the future. Shorter periods, such as a year, are inadequate to staff and develop qualified marketing managers. Longer periods, such as ten years, would make marketing manpower planning too general to be of concrete value.

Internally, most companies select candidates for marketing executive development programs on the basis of on-the-job performance and potential for marketing as reflected in periodic job reviews. Externally, candidates are selected either through college recruiting or on the basis of previous experience and potential.

Periodic reviews or evaluations and close observance by superiors are the methods most commonly used to identify highly promotable marketing executives. In some companies, on the other hand, the selection of highly promotable executives is subject to the whim of the individual manager.

53

EXHIBIT 2

Persons Responsible for Determining Marketing Executive Needs

[Responsibility for determining their own marketing executive needs as stated by respondents from 40 selected large U.S. corporations]

Title	No. of Times Mentioned
Division heads	4
Corporate personnel and general division management	2
Director of marketing	2
Managers	2
Advertising director and sales	1
managers of branches	1
Assistant vice president	1
Chairman of the board and president	1
Committee (5 persons)	
Corporate personnel	1
Director of program development	1
District sales manager	1
Executive staff	1
General manager, corporate vice president, and vice president–personnel	1
General sales manager	1
Industrial departments	1
Marketing services	1
President of each division	1
Staff department (marketing personnel development)	1
No response	16
Total	40

Criteria to determine a man's potential in marketing are, in the majority of companies, applicable to most managerial positions. Most frequently mentioned as a criterion is the general term "results." Some companies use certain measurable criteria, such as sales or profit results. The danger here is that sales or profit results alone are not necessarily indicators of success in future marketing managerial positions. A few companies use no criteria. There appears to be little in the way of other specific criteria being used by industry to determine a man's potential in marketing. Such criteria as excellence as a manager—reflected in job performance, communication skill, creativity, capacity to select and train others, and past results —are generally prerequisites for managerial success.

Company representatives most frequently expressed the need for the marketing executive of the future to acquire skills and additional knowledge in each of the following areas:

- Creativity.
- Entrepreneurship, or risk taking.
- Marketing planning.
- International marketing.
- Customer orientation.
- Information management.
- Computer applications.
- Economics.
- Management and motivation of human resources.
- Salesmanship.

Increasingly sought will be marketing managers whose qualities and capabilities fit these descriptive responses:

- "Risk takers, planners, human relations skills, marketing tools (computer technology, sales planning, production scheduling), more imagination and ideas."
- "Customer-oriented, understanding of economics of industry and of the workforce."
- "Perceptivity (recognizes change), entrepreneurship, global attitude, aptitude for planning, and a generalist."
- "Computer analysis, systems control, more sophisticated individual."
- "Customer knowledge, knowledge of economic conditions, more than a minimum knowledge of mathematics, social graces."
- "Quantitative (EDP) skills, information management,

market planning, application of scientific method to problem solving."

- "Understanding of the computer and its applications, more knowledge in depth of overseas markets, a more sophisticated understanding of advanced corporate financing."
- "Entrepreneurship, techno-economic comprehension, merchandising skill, and customer comprehension."

Although the particular type of industry in question usually had some relationship to the qualifications that would be required, there was on the whole a considerable amount of agreement.

A study [4] on the subject of preparing business leaders for the future substantiates many of the qualifications listed. Among the requirements stressed by the top executives interviewed by the authors of the study were effective staffing; broader responsibilities in governmental, social, and political spheres; more long-range planning; adaptation to changing environment; and more attention to human relations.

Seventy percent of the companies surveyed believe that their current programs will be successful in developing future qualifications, although a sizable number indicate that their programs need some strengthening to do the job required. On the other hand, 30 percent of the companies do not feel that their present programs will be successful in developing future qualifications. Moreover, it should be noted, the majority rate their current program neither good nor excellent.

Most of the companies feel that on-the-job training will contribute most toward insuring maximum development of marketing executives. When asked how they would go about developing marketing managers to meet the challenges of the next decade, the following verbatim responses were given:

[4] Bond, Floyd A., Dick A. Leabo, and Alfred W. Swinyard, *Preparation for Business Leadership—Views of Top Executives,* Michigan Business Reports, Graduate School of Business Administration, The University of Michigan, Ann Arbor, Michigan, 1964, p. 24.

- "By diligent screening of personnel and by on-the-job training."
- "Give men opportunities to work in areas where things are happening on the job."
- "Exposure and practice."
- "Same way but do it better."
- "Maximum encouragement to become innovative thinkers. Exposure to research and development thinking."

GENERAL OBSERVATIONS

Eighty percent of the current company marketing executive development programs and practices studied are not aimed in a clear-cut or specific manner at achieving their objective: developing marketing executives. Although those respondents indicating that they had such a program actually believed they did, a closer look revealed the true situation. Their programs are predominantly sales personnel development programs aimed at developing salesmen and sales managers or are general management programs aimed at developing future managers for the company. In these latter programs, sales orientation and sales experience generally are stressed as prerequisites for future managerial development.

The basic approach followed by many firms in developing marketing executives is the same approach used to train other key people in the organization. These personnel development programs follow a general pattern. They utilize in-company training courses, devices, and methods, and the majority resort to a number of development programs sponsored by outside educational institutions and professional associations. Various marketing executive development programs that exist within these outside groups are described in Chapters 6 and 7.

In practice, some programs for developing marketing executives have been outstandingly successful. They are looked upon by their companies as the most logical method of producing a continuing supply of talented marketing executives. But this situation does not always prevail. In fact, some successful programs tend to be emulated to a degree; thus what has worked well in the past for some companies tends to be extended into the future in other companies. Also, because certain companies demonstrate marketing superiority, there is a tendency to assume that their development programs must be superior.

Many companies, it must be admitted, are satisfied that their programs are adequately constructed to meet the marketing challenges of tomorrow. This may represent a dangerous complacency with the status quo in terms of the development of marketing executives. Such companies appear satisfied that their programs provide the generalized experiences and knowledge needed by the future manager of marketing.

And yet only 20 percent of the corporations surveyed had programs designed for developing marketing executives. This fact is especially significant because it reveals the thinking and practices of a substantial number of so-called blue chip companies and of many leaders in the industrial and nonindustrial fields.

DEVELOPMENT—WHOSE RESPONSIBILITY?

Companies should make every effort to assist the current or aspiring marketing executive in the acquisition of the skills and knowledge that he will need to equip himself to successfully meet the challenges of the future. At the very least, companies should provide the proper climate for development by encouraging the recognition of the necessity for continuing self-development among the junior executives in marketing. This climate should emanate from top management and permeate down through each of the levels of management. In this way, management will be able to give to this training the importance it deserves. The executives of the company must be kept constantly aware of the necessity for current and aspiring executives to acquire new skills and knowledge to meet the changing trends.

Depending upon its resources, each company should provide development opportunities within as well as outside the organization. The nature of these opportunities will vary, of course, depending on the size of the company, the number of employees, the physical and financial resources of the company, and many other factors. For example, a large company may provide an extensive formal training program within the organization. It may also send the current or aspiring marketing executive to outside courses and programs offered by professional associations, such as the American Management Association, and executive development programs offered by universities, such as Harvard.

On the other hand, a small or medium-sized company may concentrate on on-the-job training. It may offer only an occasional conference or seminar on a particular marketing subject—such as international marketing. This company may not be able to afford to send its trainees to outside courses or programs, but it should encourage individual participation in outside development activities whenever possible.

The burden of assisting the marketing executive to equip himself with the knowledge and skills that will be needed to meet the challenges of the future is a joint responsibility of the individual himself and the company. While company action must be initiated whenever possible, the individual—through personal action—must pace his own self-development.

Although it has been said that all development is self-development, the knowledge explosion in the years ahead will place increased emphasis on formal company action in the area of marketing executive development. The rapidity of change, the scarcity of marketing talent in the 30-to-45 age bracket in the next decade, and the increasing application of new skills and knowledge to the marketing function will accent the need for formal executive development action by companies large and small.

In this light, it would be unfair to place the entire burden on personal action by the practicing or aspiring market executive. It is truly a joint responsibility.

It is quite evident that companies must play a major role in the development of the marketing executive of the future. Indeed, it is in their interest to do so. Increased emphasis will necessarily be placed on formal development programs— and it is the companies themselves that will reap the greatest benefits from them.

5

A Company Program
Under the Development
Planning Concept

The development program for the product manager's job at Company *B,* under the development planning concept (referred to in Chapter 4), receives a more detailed scrutiny in the following pages. In essence, this concept is a process to identify and accelerate the preparation of an individual for a future position in order to meet future organization and manpower needs. Items 1 through 4 describe in depth the planning phases outlined in Exhibit 3.

1. POSITION REQUIREMENTS

KEY RESULTS EXPECTED

- The protection, strengthening, and building of the product's franchise through development of creative marketing plans.
- The contribution to the achievement of the product's volume

(text continues on page 64)

EXHIBIT 3

Development Planning for Future Position

Future Position Title: _____

Name of Individual: _____

PHASE 1: POSITION REQUIREMENTS

Knowledge of position requirements is prerequisite to determining individual requirements in order to screen candidates for future position openings. Following is a summary of the major responsibilities of a specific position as seen by management:

Purpose: Why the job exists and key results expected.

Major responsibilities in position: What jobholder does.

Organization to be managed: Positions to be supervised.

Level and purpose of contacts: Groups worked with inside or outside the company and reasons why.

Salary: _____

Points: _____

PHASE 2: INDIVIDUAL REQUIREMENTS

Determining individual requirements is important as a base for identifying and screening possible candidates for the position. The following is a summary of the individual requirements of candidates for the position as outlined by management:

Work experience and knowledge:
    a. What candidate should have done.
    b. Kind and depth of experience desired.

Major accomplishments: Results he should have achieved.

Education: Formal preparation, including special courses desired.

Job interests and preferences: Sources of job satisfaction important to individual in this position.

Skills and personal abilities: Personal work methods necessary to progress in this position.

EXHIBIT 3 (*concluded*)

PHASE 3: INDIVIDUAL QUALIFICATIONS

An analysis of the individual's qualifications should indicate the experiences needed—and the extent required—for an individual to qualify for this specific position. The following development needs are based on analysis of individual requirements and individual qualifications:

Has	*Needs*

Work experience and knowledge:
  a. What he has done.
  b. Kind and depth of experience.
Major accomplishments: Results he has
  achieved.
Education: Formal preparation, including special courses.
Job interests and preferences: Sources
  of job satisfaction.
Skills and personal abilities: How he
  works, personal work methods which
  have contributed to his progress.
Salary: _____
Points: _____

PHASE 4: PLANNED EXPERIENCES

Planned development experiences can be geared, through sequence and timing, to the needs of the organization and the individual. Following are activities on and off the job which provide needed learning experiences for the individual to be prepared for a position:

Company division programs and job-oriented activities: Job rotation, task force assignments, field trips, and special assignments, for example.

Company corporate program: Company-sponsored programs and seminars on selected subjects, among others.

Noncompany programs: Sponsored by professional groups and associations, universities, and others.

and profit objectives through integrated implementation of marketing plans.
· The strengthening of the communication to the consumer of the product's selling message through the stimulation and utilization of advertising skills and services.
· The sharpening of the product's marketing strategies and techniques through the stimulation of creative action.
· The broadening of the product's market potential through the identification and exploitation of innovative opportunities.

MAJOR RESPONSIBILITIES IN POSITION

Marketing plans: Develop product philosophy and marketing plans; coordinate the implementation of approved marketing plans; review and analyze effectiveness of marketing plans; maintain product history.

Profit plan: Develop profit plan objectives on unit and dollar volume, media, and deal expenses; review and analyze performance of these profit plan objectives.

Consumer and factory sales volume: Review and analyze sales trends by market (share of market, past sales, competitive activities, promotional activities, survey data) ; develop volume and share objectives; evaluate progress to volume budget.

Distribution and inventory (trade and consumer) : Determine distribution and inventory objectives required for product; review and analyze distribution, out-of-stock, inventory levels, and so on.

Consumer and trade promotion: Develop promotion plans to meet objectives; follow through on execution of promotion plans; develop and review usage and effectiveness of sales promotion materials; establish controls to measure effectiveness of promotional programs and evaluate findings.

Advertising:
  a. Agency: Direct and evaluate performance and contribution of advertising agency to overall marketing objectives; identify and interpret approved marketing objectives and plans and division philosophies to advertising agency; implement system of controls to review and analyze agency billings versus estimates; stimulate agency's creative efforts.
  b. Copy: Develop copy strategy for product; direct agency

64

execution of approved copy strategy; evaluate effectiveness of copy; review and clear copy and commercial submission for conformity to company policy.

   c. Media: Develop media strategy; coordinate and direct agency implementation of media strategy; analyze and evaluate effectiveness of media.

Pricing: Review and analyze pricing factors; develop plans for pricing changes as required.

Product and package development:

   a. Product: Develop and coordinate exploratory action to improve product convenience, performance, and overall consumer acceptance; establish and direct program for evaluation of product versus competition; coordinate the development of product quality and cost improvements and line extensions; plan and implement introduction of improved products and line extensions.

   b. Package: Plan the development and execution of package, label, and shipping carton design.

Marketing research: Identify the need for market research; coordinate the planning and implementation of all marketing research projects; evaluate findings as required.

Product publicity: Direct use of product publicity; evaluate results of publicity programs.

Personnel: Participate in selection of personnel; train and develop assigned personnel.

Other: Maintain effective controls for all budgeted items; execute special assignments as directed; plan and conduct product meetings for sales and other areas as required.

ORGANIZATIONS TO BE MANAGED

When assigned, associate, assistant product manager(s) and product assistant(s), secretary.

LEVEL AND PURPOSE OF CONTACTS

Contact	*Purpose*
Marketing manager	Review objectives, seek approval on recommendations, review results, discuss status of business and secure advice.
Advertising and merchandising manager	
Product group managers	

Contact	Purpose
Other product managers	Exchange marketing ideas and experiences.
Division	
Sales	Identify sales problems and opportunities, keep posted on field activities, and coordinate activities on objectives.
Sales planning and promotion	Coordinate development of promotion plans and evaluation of results.
Technical research	Identify opportunities for product improvement, line extensions, cost reductions.
Market research	Obtain, analyze and interpret market and consumer data.
Operations	Exchange information on production scheduling, and on product quality, and coordinate plans.
Personnel	Utilize specialized services in the selection, training, and development of people.
Financial	Submit and acquire financial data.
Corporate	
Corporate marketing	Coordinate media; consult with other available services, such as advertising, research, distribution sales service, and so on.
Company kitchens	Develop recipes, check copy, handle consumer complaints; coordinate product publicity.
Packaging	Initiate requests for new or revised packaging designs or for new concepts to be tested.
Purchasing	Procure materials for promotions, advertising.
Law	Obtain legal counsel and clearance.

Contact	Purpose
International	Exchange information and experiences.
Advertising agency	Work with agency to accomplish marketing plans and programs.
Trade and consumer	Keep informed on needs and opportunities.
	Get first-hand information helpful in identifying needs and opportunities.

2. INDIVIDUAL REQUIREMENTS (DESIRABLE QUALIFICATIONS)

EXPERIENCE AND KNOWLEDGE

The following qualifications cover a wide range of experience and knowledge and should serve as selection and training guidelines rather than as mandatory requirements:

- Participation in development and execution of marketing plans for consumer products.
- Experience in analysis and planning work.
- Experience in directing and motivating people.
- Participation in product or package planning, market testing, and national introduction.
- Knowledge of and experience working with or for an advertising agency.
- Knowledge of advertising measurement techniques.
- Experience in developing and evaluating advertising copy and media strategy and plans.
- Experience in developing and executing consumer promotions.
- Knowledge of promotional techniques.
- Knowledge of marketing research services and techniques.
- Knowledge of and experience with financial controls.
- Knowledge of sales operations and distribution processes.
- Experience in field selling.
- Knowledge of corporate organization procedures and practices.
- Knowledge of grocery trade.
- Knowledge of production processes and problems.

MAJOR ACCOMPLISHMENTS

The following qualifications cover a wide range of accomplishments in which there has been a degree of participation and should serve as evaluation guidelines rather than as mandatory requirements:

- Developed and implemented an effective marketing plan.
- Identified business-building opportunities and developed successful programs to take advantage of them.
- Assisted in development of successful new product introductions.
- Evidenced organizational and planning ability to control several projects simultaneously.
- Demonstrated good judgment in selection and development of advertising, merchandising, and promotion programs.
- Successfully coordinated a product's volume budget planning and implementation with sales area.
- Successfully planned and executed advertising campaign.
- Successfully coordinated several functions, pulling together several activities or groups to a desirable conclusion.
- Demonstrated a competitive spirit.
- Developed and executed one or more major product promotions.
- Effectively trained personnel.

EDUCATION

College graduate, economics or marketing major preferred; M.B.A. desirable but not essential.

JOB INTERESTS AND PREFERENCES

General marketing management of consumer products; overall activities of business and people; working with ideas, numbers, trends, analyses; problem solving; doing as well as planning.

SKILLS AND PERSONAL ABILITIES

- Demonstrates sound business judgment and recognizes long-term impact of decisions and recommendations.
- Identifies problems quickly and can adapt plans and programs to solve these problems.
- Develops and maintains sound relationships with business associates.

- Displays numerical ability and facility with arithmetical computations and interpretation of findings.
- Recognizes and translates business trends and developments into opportunities for profit.
- Demonstrates strong follow-through skills.
- Shows willingness to attempt new approaches.
- Recognizes need for change and initiates action.
- Stimulates and exploits innovations.
- Directs, stimulates, and coordinates, with or without authority, to obtain desired results.
- Able to work free of direction, executing or implementing basic policy decisions without day-to-day supervision.
- Communicates his ideas and thinking effectively to others.
- Displays creative skills.

3. INDIVIDUAL QUALIFICATIONS (PLANNED EXPERIENCES GUIDE)

COMPANY DIVISION PROGRAMS AND JOB-ORIENTED ACTIVITIES

Desirable qualifications (in *italics*) are to be developed through training opportunities provided by division as follows:

- *Participation in development and execution of marketing plans for consumer products.*
    - a. Limited responsibility on the job with continuing supervision at earliest opportunity after employment.
    - b. Responsibility for execution where authority can be delegated on a continuing basis during fiscal year.

- *Experience in analysis and planning work.*
    - a. Responsibilities; that is, objectives for fiscal planning within day-to-day assignment.
    - b. Job rotation to financial planning and analysis group for a limited period.

- *Experience in directing and motivating people.*
    - a. Responsibility for assigned trainees in product group, plus other subordinates as assigned.
    - b. Responsibility to coordinate product activities *through* sales, production, technical and market research, agency, and so on.
    - c. Assignment as supervisor in any related organization (sales, market research, financial department).

· *Participation in product/package planning, market testing, and national introduction.*
    a. Assignment at earliest opportunity to "task force" (within division or corporation) responsible for introducing, or studying possibility of introducing, a new product, revised package, and so on.
    b. Assignment to study, analyze, and recommend changes to existing product, packaging or product mix (quality).

· *Knowledge of and experience working with or for an advertising agency.*

· *Knowledge of advertising measurement techniques.*

· *Experience in developing and evaluating advertising copy and media strategy and plans.*
Advertising agency assignment (see item 4, "Planned Experiences").

· *Experience in developing and executing promotions.*

· *Knowledge of promotional techniques.*
Assignment in product group as promotion *contact* under close direction to gain knowledge such as:
    a. Company philosophy of promotions.
    b. Planning of promotions.
    c. Selection of type, amount, coverage, timing.
    d. Implementation and coordination of promotions: What to do, who does it, through whom, when.
    e. Evaluation of effectiveness of promotions.
    f. Planned field trips to measure the above factors "on the spot."

· *Knowledge of marketing research service and techniques.*
Assignment in product group responsible for frequent contact with marketing research on various projects, such as: volume estimates, consumer attitude, research (motivational, media, copy, promotion).

· *Knowledge of and experience with financial controls.*
    a. Assignment in product group responsible under close direction for participating in the profit plan.
    b. Responsibility for reviewing all agency and other suppliers' billings and maintaining close liaison with financial personnel to assure proper controls and approvals.

    c. Temporary assignment to controller's area to gain experience and knowledge.

· *Knowledge of sales operations and distribution processes.*
· *Experience in field selling.*
    a. Assignment in product group responsible for coordination with sales and production management of related promotion activities to include timing, stocks, and production level time.
    b. Field sales assignment (see item 4, "Planned Experiences").
    c. Temporary assignment to a distribution-sales services division location for a limited period.

· *Knowledge of corporate organization procedures and practices.*
Indoctrination program at time of employment to familiarize with division and corporate organizations and acquire knowledge of company practices and procedures and where and whom to contact for assistance.

· *Knowledge of grocery trade.*
Field trips, trade publications, contact with sales personnel.

Assignment to field sales organization and distribution-sales services division operation.

· *Knowledge of production processes and problems.*
Indoctrination program at employment.

Assignment in product group with responsibility for coordinating activities with production management.

COMPANY CORPORATE PROGRAMS

Desirable qualifications (in *italics*) are to be developed through the following programs administered by corporate marketing:

· *Participation in development and execution of marketing plans for consumer products.*
Seminar Workshop Program: *Key Factors in Product Planning.*

· *Experience in analysis and planning work.*

· *Experience in directing and motivating people.*
Depending upon number of individuals with these identified needs, company seminars could be developed concerning: com-

pany personnel policies and principles and approaches to selection, training, and compensation.

· *Participation in product/package planning, market testing, and national introduction.*

As above, seminars could be developed concerning:

a. Product/package planning, market testing, and introduction. Material should include company experience, good and bad, and would require study of problem and recommended action.

b. Methods, techniques, and so on, dealing with product/package planning, market testing and introduction of new product by agency or research personnel.

· *Experience in developing and executing promotions.*

· *Knowledge of promotional techniques.*

a. Company seminar dealing with promotion experiences, good and bad, conducted by company sales and marketing managers.

b. Company seminar reviewing the pros and cons of promotional activities conducted by research service organization.

· *Knowledge of marketing research service and techniques.*
Company seminar on products being researched and the role of marketing research in the marketing mix conducted by corporate marketing research.

· *Knowledge of and experience with financial controls.*
Company seminar dealing with financial problems in product management, such as return on funds, margins, advertising vs. promotion.

· *Knowledge of sales operations and distribution processes.*

· *Experience in field selling.*
Company seminars showing impact on field operations of products' merchandising efforts in relation to scheduling, handling, and giving customer desired service.

· *Knowledge of corporate organization procedures and practices.*
Company seminar dealing with overall practices, policies, and organization of departments relating to product manager.

- *Knowledge of grocery trade.*
  Company seminar with grocery trade leaders participating.

- *Knowledge of production processes and problems.*
  Company seminar with participation by corporate manufacturing and engineering personnel to cover such subjects as new or revised processes, production scheduling, inventory control, distribution patterns.

NONCOMPANY PROGRAMS

Desirable qualifications (in *italics*) to be developed through the following programs of outside organizations:

- *Participation in development and execution of marketing plans for consumer products.*
  AMERICAN MANAGEMENT ASSOCIATION—*Seminars:* Pricing, Marketing, New Products, Marketing Planning. *Courses:* Management Course, Marketing Course, Advanced Course in Marketing Management.
  AMERICAN MARKETING ASSOCIATION—Annual National Conference.

- *Experience in analysis and planning work.*
  AMERICAN MANAGEMENT ASSOCIATION—*Seminars:* Marketing Planning and Control, Marketing Research, Advertising, Marketing Management. *Courses:* Management Course, Product and Brand Management Course.
  SALES AND MARKETING EXECUTIVES-INTERNATIONAL—Executive Development Program.
  ADVERTISING FEDERATION OF AMERICA—Annual Harvard Seminar for Advanced Management in Advertising and Marketing.
  COLUMBIA UNIVERSITY—Marketing Management Program.

- *Experience in directing and motivating people.*
  AMERICAN MANAGEMENT ASSOCIATION—*Seminars:* Marketing Management. *Courses:* Management Course, Executive Action Course, Marketing Course.
  SALES AND MARKETING EXECUTIVES-INTERNATIONAL—Executive Development Program.
  COLUMBIA UNIVERSITY—Marketing Management Program.

- *Participation in product/package planning, market testing, and national introduction.*

AMERICAN MANAGEMENT ASSOCIATION—*Seminars:* New Products, Product Planning; Finding, Screening and Appraising New Products. *Courses:* Advanced Course in Marketing Management, Packaging Management Course, Product Planning and Development Course.

AMERICAN MARKETING ASSOCIATION—Annual National Conference.

COLUMBIA UNIVERSITY—Marketing Management Program.

· *Knowledge of and experience working with or for an advertising agency.*

· *Knowledge of advertising measurement techniques.*

· *Experience in developing and evaluating advertising copy and media strategy and plans.*

AMERICAN MANAGEMENT ASSOCIATION—*Seminars:* Advertising and Sales Promotion, Advertising, Product Manager. *Courses:* Advertising Management Courses.

ADVERTISING AGE—Annual Summer Workshop.

ADVERTISING FEDERATION OF AMERICA—Annual Harvard Seminar for Advanced Management in Advertising and Marketing.

ASSOCIATION OF NATIONAL ADVERTISERS—Annual Spring Meeting.

· *Experience in developing and executing promotions.*

· *Knowledge of promotional techniques.*

AMERICAN MANAGEMENT ASSOCIATION—*Seminar:* Advertising and Sales Promotion.

· *Knowledge of marketing research service and techniques.*

AMERICAN MANAGEMENT ASSOCIATION—*Seminars:* New Products, Marketing Planning and Control, Marketing Research. *Courses:* Advanced Course in Marketing Management, Marketing Research Course.

SALES AND MARKETING EXECUTIVES-INTERNATIONAL—Executive Development Program.

· *Knowledge of and experience with financial controls.*

AMERICAN MANAGEMENT ASSOCIATION—*Seminars:* Marketing, Fundamentals of Finance and Accounting for Nonfinancial Executives, Marketing Planning and Control, Marketing Research. *Courses:* Advanced Course in Marketing Management, Marketing Course, Product and Brand Management Course.

ASSOCIATION OF NATIONAL ADVERTISERS—Annual Spring Meeting.

SALES AND MARKETING EXECUTIVES-INTERNATIONAL—Executive Development Program.

· *Knowledge of sales operations and distribution processes.*

· *Experience in field selling.*

AMERICAN MANAGEMENT ASSOCIATION—*Seminars:* Marketing Management, Advertising and Sales Promotion. *Courses:* Marketing Management Course, Marketing Course.

· *Knowledge of corporate organization procedures and practices.*

AMERICAN MANAGEMENT ASSOCIATION—*Courses:* Organization Planning and Control, Corporate Long-Range Planning.

· *Knowledge of grocery trade.*

AMERICAN MANAGEMENT ASSOCIATION—*Courses:* Course in Antitrust and Trade Practice Regulations.

· *Knowledge of production processes and problems.*

AMERICAN MANAGEMENT ASSOCIATION—*Seminar:* Production and Inventory Control.

4. PLANNED EXPERIENCES

In addition to the preceding Planned Experiences Guide, further guidelines are provided to assist in the development of product managers for these particular qualifications:

1. Knowledge of and experience working with or for an advertising agency.
2. Knowledge of sales operations and distribution processes. Experience in field selling.
3. Knowledge of marketing research service and techniques.

While these experiences are designed primarily for new people, they are applicable to all personnel who may have need for knowledge of one or more of the subjects. The selection of experiences, method of implementation, and duration of the exposure to a particular experience is a responsibility of the operating area to which the individual is assigned. In providing the experience, it is suggested that those concerned perform the following functions:

Division marketing management: Schedule and assign individuals; meet periodically with participants to review their progress; assign an appropriate individual to guide execution of these experiences on a continuing basis; evaluate the effectiveness of the experiences and communicate suggestions for improvement to corporate marketing.

Agency, sales, and marketing research management: Provide necessary experiences, as requested; review with their personnel the purpose of these planned experiences and their responsibilities; assign a point of contact for company product management participants during their experiences.

Participants: Report to assigned manager to review progress, problems, and suggestions; submit a written report to division marketing management on their agency and sales experiences.

Corporate marketing: Act as liaison with agencies and other services in the preparation and presentation of training material with broad application for use with company personnel. There may be instances where duplication of effort and expense can be avoided if requirements in this area are coordinated. Also, corporate marketing will periodically discuss with the divisions their application and evaluation of these experiences in achieving the objective of providing adequate training for men, particularly college recruits, in need of the required knowledge.

ADVERTISING AGENCY EXPERIENCE

Purpose: (1) To provide individuals with knowledge of an advertising agency. (2) To provide insight into the operation of an agency to maximize the opportunities for stimulating their effective contribution.

Prerequisites: Should have an understanding of company marketing organization and procedures, company-agency relationships and expectations, advertising terminology, and a textbook knowledge of the advertising agency business. Suggested material for reading: division advertising plans, company advertising policies and procedures, company-agency billing policies, agency-product management relationships, other reference material to be specified by division.

76

Suggested schedule: This planned experience can be arranged in keeping with the workload of the division and the agency. The agency experience could be accomplished in one assignment of several weeks duration, or at intervals, in conjunction with on-the-job responsibilities requiring work at the agencies.

Scheduling will depend, to some extent, on activities relating to company's products being available in each agency for observation and participation by the company product management personnel assigned to that agency. This will assure productive utilization of the agency's facilities and the company trainee's time.

Agency departments to be covered: In developing knowledge of agency operations, it is suggested that the individual be exposed to the duties and responsibilities of each of the following major departments as well as of other functions (plans boards, product groups, and so on). Actual participation in work assignments in one or more of these departments also might be productive in the training process:

Executive	Research
Copy	Traffic
Art	Accounting
Print production	Legal
Commercial production	Publicity
Media	Contact
Television programming	

FIELD SALES EXPERIENCE

Purpose: (1) To provide knowledge of company field sales operations and distribution channels. (2) To provide experience in field selling.

Prerequisites: Participants should have understanding of company sales organization structure (headquarters and field) and responsibilities; product management-sales relationships; and division products, policies, practices, and so on. They should have read the following: division marketing plan (s), division sales manual, company position requirements of field sales positions, other reference material to be specified by division.

Suggested schedule: This experience should require a 6- to 12-month time period, depending upon the individual. It is desirable to schedule it as early in his career as possible. Following is a list of activities to which an individual should be exposed and the type of knowledge he should endeavor to assimilate during his training period. The time required for each activity will be influenced by circumstances and the individual's progress rate.

Activity	*To Gain Knowledge of—*
Orientation to sales function and responsibilities.	Division headquarters operations.
	Field sales operations.
	Sales department philosophy of operations.
	Competitive and trade factors.
	Responsibilities of sales management.
	Responsibilities of the account manager, sales supervisor, and sales representative.
	Scheduling and control.
	Procedures.
Retail account selling as sales representative.	Distribution, pricing, shelf location, displays, competitive activity, point of sale material, promotions, and deals.
	Retailer gross margins, rate of turnover, profit contribution.
	Trade personnel handling.
	Variations in brand franchises.
	Application of selling techniques and principles.
	Implementation of division plans.
	Utilization of customers (retail and direct) facilities.
Direct account handling as sales representative.	Direct account responsibility in terms of the above.
Orientation to distribution-sales service division functions and responsibilities.	Order handling, billing, warehousing, credit control, and so on.

MARKETING RESEARCH EXPERIENCE

Purpose: To provide individuals with knowledge of marketing research services and techniques.

Prerequisites: Participants should have some understanding of role of marketing research in marketing of company products. They should have read: selected research studies pertaining to divisions' products; research reports of such services as Nielsen, Market Research Corporation of America (*MRCA*), and so on; other reference material to be specified by division.

Suggested procedure: Individuals in need of this experience can gain knowledge through sessions on the following subjects by division or corporate marketing research personnel.

Organization of marketing research function: In division; in corporate marketing.

Marketing research areas:
1. Market research data sources
   · Nielsen Food Index.
   · Market Research Corporation of America.
   · Use and attitude studies.
   · Sales analysis.
   · Government marketing data sources.

2. Market testing
   · Market potentials.
   · Market characteristics.
   · Audits.
   · Shelving.
   · Pricing.
   · Packaging.
   · Store positioning.
   · Media allocation.

3. Product testing
   · Types of tests: concept, immediate preference, home placement, extended use.
   · Facilities for testing: store, cafeteria, luncheon groups, homemaker testing, mail panels, personal placement.

4. Packaging research
   · Physical characteristics.

79

   · Design.
   · Label.
   · Directions.
   · Performance.

5. Advertisement research
   · Copy testing.
   · Media research.
   · Measures of effectiveness: recall (Gallup & Robinson, Starch), attitude change (Schwerin), audience measurements (Nielsen, Advertising Research Bureau).
   · Spending levels.
   · Gallup & Robinson Total Prime Time studies.

6. Promotion research
   · Control vs. test markets/stores.
   · Year-ago comparisons.
   · Competitive performance.

7. Miscellaneous
   · Market Research Corporation of America Menu Study.
   · Consumer polls.
   · Share of market studies.
   · Application of computer and market models.

The program just described demonstrates how one company follows a systematic approach in developing product managers. This same company applies a similar approach to other types of marketing executives, such as sales managers in manufacturing, finance, and other areas of the business. It is one way that has worked.

6

Programs and Policies
of Colleges and
Universities

A look at the current programs, philosophies, and
practices of selected colleges and universities provides an index
to the marketing education offered to the current or aspiring
marketing executive. The institutions selected were recommended by the companies surveyed as having outstanding executive development programs tailored to the needs of current
or would-be marketing executives (Exhibit 4). These institutions were also recommended for their excellent M.B.A. program by the company representatives interviewed.

A number of the corporations surveyed mentioned the following as having a superior master's program in business administration: Dartmouth College; Cornell, Indiana, Michigan,
Michigan State, New York, Ohio State, Pennsylvania, Wiscon-

EXHIBIT 4

Colleges and Universities with Company-Recommended Marketing Executive Development Programs

[Named by respondents from 40 selected large U.S. corporations as having outstanding executive development programs for developing marketing executives]

College or University	No. of Times Mentioned
Harvard University (Advanced Management Program)	9
Stanford University	4
Carnegie Institute of Technology	3
University of Chicago	3
Columbia University	2
Massachusetts Institute of Technology	1
Northwestern University	1
No response	20

sin, and Washington State universities. Several of the institutions named also offer executive development programs for marketing executives, but these programs were not singled out by the responding corporations.

Although the title of only one company-recommended program includes the term "marketing," all programs provide substantial educational content aimed at assisting the potential or present marketing executive in the acquisition of needed skills and knowledge.

Brief reviews of program content and comments provided by the persons in charge of the programs at several of the institutions surveyed reveal the philosophy of each institution.

HARVARD UNIVERSITY

At the Graduate School of Business Administration, Harvard offers an advanced management program in two 13-week sessions per year (Exhibit 5). Participants are drawn from top management or potential top management. The university also offers an annual 16-week program for management development at the Business School (Exhibit 6). For this program, participants are drawn from middle levels of management— five to ten years' experience in business is required.

The philosophy is stated by Martin V. Marshall, professor of business administration and chairman of the marketing area faculty at the Graduate School of Business Administration. It is essentially the same philosophy that underlies the regular M.B.A. program, although the time and attention devoted to marketing in the latter are necessarily greater.

> . . . Our activities in developing people for marketing have to be looked upon in quite a broad context. We are fundamentally concerned with helping men to develop so that they will be effective business administrators throughout their business careers. . . .
>
> In our marketing work, we are primarily interested in developing an understanding of what is involved in effective marketing under the longer term with special emphasis on the interrelationship between key marketing decisions and other elements of the business. Or, to put it another way, we are not

---

EXHIBIT 5

Harvard University
Advanced Management Program

SPONSOR: Graduate School of Business Administration.
DURATION: Two 13-week sessions, annually.
PARTICIPANTS: Top management or potential top management.
GROUP SIZE: 130.
PROGRAM: The content includes: Business Policy; Cost and Financial Administration; Marketing; Labor; Administrative Practices; Behavioral Sciences; Business, Society, and Individual.
TEACHING METHODS: Case, lecture, seminar, discussion, field trip.

EXHIBIT 6

Harvard University
Program for Management Development

SPONSOR: Graduate School of Business Administration.
DURATION: 16 weeks, annually.
PARTICIPANTS: Middle levels of management—10 years of business experience preferred, but 5 years experience accepted.
GROUP SIZE: Not specified.
AIM: To develop in the young manager the skills, understanding, and attitudes essential to the effective execution of administrative responsibilities.
PROGRAM: The curriculum includes: General Management, Human Behavior in Organizations, Quantitative Analysis, and Issues in Business.
TEACHING METHODS: Lecture, study.

interested in teaching men detailed existing practices, or the best research practices, etc. We are interested in developing the capacity of men to deal with what we have come to call the concept of the marketing mix. . . .

With regard to the challenges of the 1970's, our principal thrust is to constantly keep before our men the fact that this is a changing world, that this is an uncertain world, that it is a difficult world to predict; but nonetheless, the chief responsibility of the marketer is to anticipate the future environment in which he will be living and to adapt his operations to his environment. We are asking our men to be students continuously of the social, political, competitive, governmental, technological and other forces that shape the environment in which a business must operate.

We are giving a great deal of attention to specific skills which we think men probably will need, such as mathematical skills, and a knowledge of the behavioral sciences. . . .

EXHIBIT 7

Stanford University
The Stanford Executive Program

DURATION: 8 weeks, annually.
PARTICIPANTS: Top management.
GROUP SIZE: 80 (two 40-man groups).
AIM: To develop general managers rather than specialists.
PROGRAM: The curriculum includes: Management Controls; Business, Government, and the Market System; the Economic System; Behavioral Sciences for Management; Management of Marketing; Financial Management; Business Policy.
TEACHING METHODS: Case, lecture, seminar, discussion, role playing, field trip.

STANFORD UNIVERSITY

Stanford offers an eight-week executive development program annually at the Graduate School of Business (Exhibit 7). Participants are drawn from top management and should have 15 to 20 years of experience in business. No more than two participants from the same company are permitted to attend the same session.

The philosophy of the program is expressed by its director, Robert T. Davis: "In our Executive Program we do not emphasize marketing per se, although we do have a marketing management course. Our Program is designed for General Managers rather than for functional specialists."

UNIVERSITY OF CHICAGO

The University of Chicago does not offer an executive development program specifically designed for marketing executives. The Graduate School of Business at the university, however, offers its regular Executive Program on a continuing basis, and approximately 15 to 20 percent of the managers enrolled in that program are concerned with marketing management.

The general philosophy underlying marketing offerings is stated by John E. Jeuck, professor of business administration at the Graduate School of Business:

> . . . We have for the past eight or ten years demanded a substantial amount of work in quantitative methods and behavioral sciences in our MBA Program. The School philosophy is that a maximum of about one-third of a student's total program at the MBA level may appropriately be spent in a field of concentration. This means that our students specializing in marketing will take not more than five or six courses in marketing. In most cases, a student probably takes about four such courses. We conceive marketing to be a field of application rather than a self-contained discipline, science or methodology. In our course work we concentrate on providing students an opportunity to develop an understanding of the nature of marketing problems and we try to provide the challenges associated with applying systematic theory and methodology to the solution of particular marketing problems. We have recently added two marketing courses in consumer behavior, but we do not anticipate increasing specialized offerings in any significant degree.
>
> With respect to practitioners, we do not now have any continuing program oriented specifically to marketing personnel. From time to time, we undertake special residential seminar offerings in various subjects.
>
> We have offered residential seminars for academicians interested in teaching and research in marketing, and I believe we shall probably continue to offer special interest seminars and symposia from time to time. . . .

CARNEGIE INSTITUTE OF TECHNOLOGY

Carnegie Institute of Technology offers a nine-week program for executives from upper and middle management at the

---

EXHIBIT 8

Carnegie Institute of Technology
Program for Executives

SPONSOR: Graduate School of Industrial Administration.
DURATION: 9 weeks, each spring.
PARTICIPANTS: Upper and middle management.
GROUP SIZE: 45–50.
AIM: To accelerate professional development of the manager who is expected to assume wider responsibilities while continuing high-level performance in his present assignment.
PROGRAM: *Core courses* include Corporate Strategy, Economics, Human Behavior in Organizations, and Managerial Control. *Electives* in Marketing Planning and Analysis, Production and Operations, Management of Research and Development, Management Information Systems.
TEACHING METHODS: Discussion, lecture, seminar, role playing, cases. Considerable advance reading between candidate's acceptance and actual start of classes.

Graduate School of Industrial Administration (Exhibit 8). The content of the program is an integrated whole rather than a collection of specialized courses. Its philosophy is stated by Bernard P. Goldsmith, director of management programs at the Graduate School of Industrial Administration:

In selecting each year's class, the Graduate School seeks a balance of backgrounds among executives at or near the policy-making level. Marketing executives work closely with fellow-participants from a broad variety of business fields and industries.

The Program emphasizes the General Manager's role as a policy framer, resources coordinator, and decision maker. Details of specific functions and techniques are scrutinized only to the extent that such detail will be of value to the responsible executive.

EXHIBIT 9

Columbia University

Marketing Management Program

SPONSOR: Graduate School of Business.

DURATION: 6 days, annually.

PARTICIPANTS: Senior marketing executives.

GROUP SIZE: 70.

AIM: The program is designed to help marketing executives: (1) diagnose, analyze, and solve marketing management problems from an organizationwide rather than a departmental point of view; (2) extend their grasp of the total marketing management function within its companywide setting; (3) develop a broader understanding of the impact of the economic-technological-political-social-environment on business, on marketing, and on policy decisions; (4) explore new management science techniques for analysis and control of marketing operations.

PROGRAM: Focuses on the following topics: Trends in the American Market: Challenge and Opportunity; Critical Marketing Problems of the Next Ten Years; Marketing Management at the Policy Level: Nature and Scope of the Job; Design and Implementation of Effective Marketing Programs; Managing Innovation in Marketing; New Techniques for Marketing Management: Management Science and Computers; Developing New Competences.

TEACHING METHODS: Discussion, case, study group. Guest speakers from business and government, with special experience in various phases of marketing, lead discussions in the general meetings.

Within the schedule, each participant is encouraged to avail himself of the on-campus resources to work on some broad-gauge problem from his own company. Thus, some of the men inevitably will also meet privately with faculty members known for their marketing expertise as consultants and researchers. Throughout, readings and assignments have been interwoven to brief experienced managers on the state-of-the-art and promising new developments in managerial techniques and concepts (including recent advances in marketing, of course).

COLUMBIA UNIVERSITY

Annually, Columbia University's Graduate School of Business offers a specialized six-day marketing management program for senior marketing executives (Exhibit 9).

There are no academic requirements for enrollment in the program. Participants are selected from among the applicants on the basis of policy-making experience and interest in marketing management, and an effort is made to include representatives from many kinds of industries from various parts of the country.

MASSACHUSETTS INSTITUTE OF TECHNOLOGY

A 16-week program for senior executives is offered by the Massachusetts Institute of Technology at its School of Industrial Management. Participants are drawn from upper management (Exhibit 10). M.I.T. also offers a year-long Sloan Fellowship program in executive development for middle management (Exhibit 11). Participants range between the ages of 32 and 38 and should have five to ten years' business experience in addition to a bachelor's degree.

M.I.T.'s philosophy with regard to marketing executive development is stated by John D. C. Little, associate professor and marketing group coordinator, in these terms:

EXHIBIT 10

Massachusetts Institute of Technology
Program for Senior Executives

SPONSOR: School of Industrial Management.
DURATION: 16 weeks (2 sessions), annually.
PARTICIPANTS: Upper-level managers.
GROUP SIZE: 20.
AIM: To provide the participants with an increased understanding of the executive function.
PROGRAM: The content of the program is organized around four core seminars. *Core seminars*—Economics; Finance; Organizational Behavior; The Institutional and Business Environment. *Functional seminars*—Organization; Industrial Dynamics; Personnel and Labor Relations; Controllership; Marketing; Taxation.
TEACHING METHODS: Management seminar, individual project or panel, scientific seminar, case, lecture, discussion, role playing.

Our programs are aimed at the development of general management capabilities. A number of the participants usually have marketing backgrounds and almost all are actively interested in marketing problems. However, the general educational goals are a wide knowledge of management subjects and the development of problem solving skills. As compared to other schools our marketing offerings probably have more content in quantitative methods and more emphasis on an overall systems viewpoint. This is a result of faculty strengths in these areas and of the rapidly increasing importance of these areas to marketing. We believe that the managers and marketing men who are coming up in the next five to ten years will want to be able to think effectively in these terms. However, many important marketing concepts are not quantitative and so our courses also contain a wide variety of behavioral and conceptual material relevant to marketing management.

EXHIBIT 11

Massachusetts Institute of Technology
Sloan Fellowship Program in Executive Development

SPONSOR: School of Industrial Management.
DURATION: One year.
PARTICIPANTS: Middle managers.
GROUP SIZE: 45 (15 in each seminar group).
AIM: General management development.
PROGRAM: Includes: The Economic Environment of the Firm;
   Information for Decision and Control; The Functions of
   the Firm; Management of Human Resources; The Social
   and Political Environment. Seminars are offered on: Man-
   agement and the Arts and Sciences; Plant and Management
   Visits.
TEACHING METHODS: Case, lecture, seminar, discussion, role
   playing, field trip, meeting with financial and corporate
   executives, domestic and international business and government representatives.

NORTHWESTERN UNIVERSITY

Northwestern University's School of Business sponsors a
four-week institute for management. Participants are senior
managers who are corporate officers, division heads, or policy-
level executives (Exhibit 12). Issues concurrently involving
marketing, finance, production, human relations, factors of
local and national legislation, international business activities,
business cycles, group behavior, economic controls, corporate
planning, managing technological change, the profit system,
and others are dealt with as components of an evolving program.

EXHIBIT 12

Northwestern University
Institute for Management

SPONSOR: School of Business.

DURATION: 4 weeks (2 sessions), annually.

PARTICIPANTS: Senior managers.

GROUP SIZE: 45 in each session.

AIM: The purpose of the institute is to broaden—to expose men of already established strengths to the experience of wrestling with the problems of the chief executive and to stimulate them to formulate policies respecting the responsibilities of business toward society.

PROGRAM: The faculty does not teach "subjects" but seeks to instill a discipline of thought through which the varied dimensions of management thinking are fused. The institute helps specialists become generalists, and the program may be described as mind-stretching and perspective-building.

TEACHING METHODS: Materials used center around top management thought and action. Problems considered are not confined to any particular firm or industry but are viewed from the conceptual standpoint of general managerial concern. While the educational process is not restricted to any single technique, the case discussion method is the predominant vehicle for instruction. Guest speakers from business, labor, government, and education address the group and exchange views on a wide range of topics.

Northwestern also sponsors a three-week Institute for International Management in Switzerland for officers of multinational companies—men who influence the formulation of corporate policy within an international framework (Exhibit 13). The participants represent a cross-section of functions, industries, and geographical areas. The program is conducted in English.

EXHIBIT 13

Northwestern University
Institute for International Management

SPONSOR: School of Business.
DURATION: 3 weeks, annually.
LOCATION: Switzerland.
PARTICIPANTS: Officers of international corporations.
GROUP SIZE: 30 to 35.
AIM: Emphasis is placed upon promoting an understanding of worldwide business and upon the strategy for operating in multinational markets.
PROGRAM: The institute provides a forum where men of diverse experience and background can exchange ideas on the policies and problems of conducting international business activities within a global environment. Problems considered are not confined to any particular firm or industry but are viewed from the conceptual standpoint of general managerial concern.
TEACHING METHODS: Materials used in the program center around top management thought and action. The educational process is not restricted to any single method, although the case discussion method is the prevalent vehicle for instruction. World-renowned authorities from government and business circles address the group as guest speakers and exchange views on international topics.

OVERALL PROGRAM EMPHASIS

These institutions follow a variety of approaches and philosophies in developing marketing executives. The emphasis in their executive development programs is toward developing generalists for marketing. In fact, six of the seven company-recommended programs are general management development programs for executives, in which certain aspects of marketing

93

are discussed. In addition, stress is placed on an understanding of marketing under the longer term view, of the newer quantitative concepts in marketing, and of the complex environment in which the marketing executive must operate. All the institutions—and many businessmen—agree that the marketing executive can learn the specifics on the job but that problem-solving and decision-making concepts are best learned at the university.

OTHER DEVELOPMENT OPPORTUNITIES

Institutions of higher learning in the United States offer business a variety of executive development programs in addition to those cited. Several of these programs may be of interest to firms as aids in developing marketing executives of the future.

Many colleges and universities offer regular course work on the undergraduate and graduate levels in marketing and related fields of business.[1] There are programs that dovetail almost exactly with the needs of certain executives for marketing education. For example, they offer courses in marketing research, international marketing, consumer analysis and motivation, marketing systems, computer applications in marketing —to name a few—which fit in nicely with the needs of some aspiring or current marketing executives. These courses can be taken as part of a degree program or on an individual course basis, part time or full time, depending on the needs of the individual.

A number of colleges and universities offer seminars, conferences, institutes, workshops, or evening and extension programs in the field of marketing. These nondegree programs, of shorter duration and much more specific in scope than the

[1] See Luck, David J., *Marketing Education in the United States,* Marketing Science Institute, Philadelphia, 1964.

lengthy executive development programs, are of great assistance in the development of the marketing executive.

Some executives who take these courses pay their own way, but many companies have a tuition refund plan of one type or another which is used to assist the executive who wishes to pursue courses as part of his executive development. Motivation, in most cases, must be supplied by the individual. As one study on management development points out:

> . . . The usual approach to part-time training involves encouragement and occasional guidance in the selection of programs but very little direction and nomination of individuals for training. . . . The decision to apply for these offerings usually is made by the individual manager, although his superior may guide him in this decision.[2]

In the main, the colleges and universities of the United States recognize the impact of the changing environment of business on the executive. As the importance of the marketing executive becomes more apparent and the need even more critical, it seems safe to assume that colleges and universities will increase the opportunities available for training programs which will help the marketing executive acquire the skills and knowledge he needs.

It is also apparent that a company can take advantage of the knowledge residing in the institutions of higher learning. The company can encourage its executives to participate in seminars, courses, workshops, or conferences sponsored by the institutions. And the company can call upon the institution's experts in the field of marketing for advice and counsel.

[2] Mahoney, Thomas A., *Building the Executive Team: A Guide to Management Development,* Prentice-Hall, Inc., Englewood, New Jersey, 1961, p. 243.

7

Programs and Policies of Professional Associations

Many professional associations offer courses, programs, publications, and activities—especially on the local chapter level—which dovetail with the needs of both marketing executives and companies. Four of these associations were highly recommended for their programs and practices in train-

EXHIBIT 14

Professional Associations with Company-Recommended Marketing Executive Development Programs

[Named as having outstanding programs by respondents from 40 selected large U.S. corporations]

Professional Association	No. of Times Mentioned
American Management Association	7
National Industrial Conference Board	4
Association of National Advertisers	2
American Marketing Association	1
No response	25

ing marketing executives by the companies surveyed (Exhibit 14). Their programs give an indication of the types of educational opportunities available to the marketing executive through these means.

AMERICAN MANAGEMENT ASSOCIATION

For more than 40 years, nonprofit AMA has dedicated itseelf to the purpose of providing executives with a comprehensive and continually updated program of management education. By alerting managers to rapidly developing business trends, this program enables them to stay ahead of the dynamic changes that are constantly taking place in the world of management.

The AMA program is guided by the association's board of directors, the All-AMA Planning Council, and the divisional planning councils—composed of leading managers and specialists in their respective fields—and by the individual recommendations and requests of its more than 48,000 members. With the assistance of these practical businessmen, the program aims at providing managers with an opportunity for training in an exchange of management experience.

This extensive program of management education is carried out through workshop and orientation seminars, courses, conferences, management information services, programmed instruction, periodicals, and other publications. The latter include research studies, management bulletins, and books, all covering the subject areas of the 11 AMA divisions.

AMA describes the work of one of these divisions, the Marketing Division, in these terms:

> Probably no area of management is subject to so many shifting changes and conditions as that of marketing. For this reason, sales, advertising, marketing research, and other marketing executives find it profitable to enroll in the AMA's Marketing Division and to examine trends and exchange viewpoints. The

EXHIBIT 15

American Management Association
Marketing Course

SPONSOR: Marketing Division.

DURATION: 3 one-week (Monday-Friday) units, spaced out over approximately 3 months.

PARTICIPANTS: Upper- and middle-level marketing managers.

GROUP SIZE: 60.

AIM: The course offers an opportunity to gain firm understanding of the marketing concept—the customer-oriented company—and on how to handle the forces involved in orienting the company's total management thinking, planning, and productive effort for increased volume, profit, and return on investment.

PROGRAM: Enrollment is for all three units, which are divided as follows: *Unit I*—Developing the Marketing Team: Responsibilities of Marketing Management; Objectives and Policies of Marketing Management; Marketing Activities —Marketing Research; Product Planning; Sales Training; Advertising and Sales Promotion. *Unit II*—Organizing, Planning and Controlling the Marketing Activity; Product Management; Pricing; Marketing Planning. *Unit III* —Personnel Considerations in the Marketing Activity: Communication in the Marketing Organization; Marketing Personnel Development and Administration; Sales Force Motivation, Morale and Compensation; Integration, and Evaluation of the Total Marketing Activity; Summary.

TEACHING METHODS: Lectures and discussions are supplemented by a course notebook which includes outlines of lectures, supplementary reading materials, charts, graphs, and bibliography. Case studies, project session, and group discussion. Leadership of the course is supplied by top operating executives from industry, who conduct sessions in their own fields of specialization.

Division sponsors conferences, seminars, and other meeting activities in which all aspects of current marketing management are covered. These include such problems as the selection and training of salesmen, marketing planning, pricing, promotional methods, the development and launching of new products—and, not least of all, the improvement of sales management itself.

Periodically, AMA offers some type of marketing program to fill various knowledge needs of practically every type of marketing executive. Its basic marketing course is designed for executives in the upper and middle levels of management with substantial business experience and background (Exhibit 15).

NATIONAL INDUSTRIAL CONFERENCE BOARD

NICB is a nonprofit research and service organization with a strong business orientation. It publishes a great deal of material on company practices and techniques in marketing management, product management, sales management, marketing research, and advertising.

In the fall, NICB holds its three-day marketing conference, the largest of its kind, in New York City. The purpose of the conference is to promote better marketing practices and to stimulate the thinking of practitioners by bringing together knowledgeable marketing leaders. These leaders draw on their own experiences and those of their companies to discuss practical approaches in three general areas: top marketing management, sales management, and marketing staff activities. Over two or three years, the conferences are likely to cover most key areas of current interest to marketing management.

The sessions at the annual marketing conference are generally varied. Questions explored at a recent conference included: How can the company adapt its operations to changing market needs? What are some practical rules for achieving planned diversification? What can management do to improve the quality of marketing decision making? What does the company's chief executive expect from marketing and the marketing manager? Other subjects discussed were advanced techniques in marketing, marketing research, and advertising; sales communications; and sales specialization. NICB also holds an annual spring marketing conference, which alternates between West Coast and Midwest locations.

ASSOCIATION OF NATIONAL ADVERTISERS

ANA is a nonprofit service organization operated for mutual advantage by some 700 companies whose products and services are marketed nationally or regionally. The association describes itself as—

> . . . the only association concerned solely with the interests of the users of advertising. Since 1910, in that capacity, ANA has rendered practical services to member companies directed toward helping them secure maximum returns from their advertising expenditures. ANA helps members stretch their advertising dollars; provides useful and timely information not available elsewhere; assists in the training and development of member advertising and marketing executives; and communicates advertisers' practices and attitudes to agencies, media and other suppliers of advertising services, as well as to the public and government.

To assist in the training and development of member advertising and marketing executives, ANA established the Advertising Management Development Committee. Roland P. Campbell, chairman of this committee, describes its purpose:

> Over the years ANA has recognized as one of its primary responsibilities the provision of assistance to member companies in the training and development of their advertising executives. If a company's advertising is to make its maximum contribution to growth and profits, the responsible executives must be as well-grounded in management attitudes and approaches as

in the skills of their craft. With this in mind, ANA invested more than $200,000 in the late 1950's in the preparation of its seven-volume series of Advertising Management Guidebooks and has continued to expand this basic library with supplementary material including the recent books entitled *Defining Advertising Goals for Measured Advertising Results, Management and Advertising Problems,* and *Advertising and Competition.*

As a reflection of the constantly growing demands on the marketing and advertising functions, a membership survey recently indicated that the Association might well step up further its activity in helping member advertising executives accelerate their managerial development. Toward this end, the Committee on Advertising Management Development was formed, and Dean Albert W. Frey of the University of Pittsburgh's Graduate School of Business was retained to assist in preparing a curriculum and in coordinating the program.

The initial seminar was held in March 1963 at the Westchester Country Club, with an attendance of 60 participants representing 55 member companies of ANA. The response to this seminar was so favorable as to warrant additional ANA Advanced Advertising Management seminars.

In addition, ANA's general meetings, special-subject workshops, and regional conferences have provided channels for the exposure of new advertising management concepts and procedures. On the whole, ANA—through its various activities— seems to have an appreciable impact on the development of advertising managerial personnel for marketing.

AMERICAN MARKETING ASSOCIATION

The American Marketing Association fosters scientific research, study, and education in all phases of marketing and encourages idea exchange between members with similar interests. The association has in the United States and in other countries over 13,000 members who share a common interest in the factual approach to the solution of marketing problems. This description of its activities is given by the association:

National and regional conferences are held each year at which leaders of marketing thought are provided a forum to express their points of view. Local chapter meetings, seminars, and workshops provide additional opportunities for the exchange of useful information.

This program is directed toward practitioners, top management and academicians so that the greatest possible coordination is effected. The fact that the membership has representatives from both the teaching and business fields affords the unique opportunity to our members of combining the theories of marketing with its actual practice.

In addition, the association publishes two quarterlies. Written for marketing practitioners, businessmen interested in marketing, and teachers and students of marketing, the *Journal of Marketing* makes available information about new marketing discoveries, techniques, ideas, trends, and related subjects. The *Journal of Marketing Research* contains articles on the application of problem-solving methods and techniques to the solution of marketing problems.

The American Marketing Association performs few other activities to develop marketing executives. On the other hand, local chapter activities—seminars, conferences, and workshops —provide considerable assistance to marketing practitioners in those areas where the chapters are particularly active. The New York chapter, for example, does an excellent job in this area. Its monthly publication is very valuable since many members are unable to attend the local chapter meetings. Each issue contains a number of well-written articles on vital subjects from an application point of view.

OTHER PROFESSIONAL ORGANIZATIONS

A number of other professional associations can be of assistance in developing the skills and knowledge of the practicing

EXHIBIT 16

American Advertising Federation
Seminar in Marketing Management and Advertising

DURATION: 2 weeks.
PARTICIPANTS: Executives in responsible positions in advertising and other phases of marketing.
GROUP SIZE: Limited.
AIM: To provide executives with the opportunity to study, analyze, and discuss marketing, advertising, and related policies and problems from the viewpoint of top management.
PROGRAM: The content is designed to expose participants to a variety of actual business situations; to have them concentrate on problems that demand careful analysis of facts and the development of imaginative solutions; to provide fresh insights into the entire complex of facts that affect decision making; and to review problems and functions in marketing management and advertising.
TEACHING METHODS: Discussion, case, lecture, study group.

or aspiring marketing executive. Among these associations are: American Advertising Federation, which sponsors an annual seminar at Harvard's Graduate School of Business Administration (Exhibit 16); Sales Executives Club of New York; Sales and Marketing Executives-International, which conducts an annual program at Syracuse University (Exhibit 17); Association of Industrial Advertisers; and Public Relations Society of America Incorporated.

Several professional marketing organizations assist indirectly in the development of marketing executives. Included among these are: American Association of Advertising Agencies, a leading national advertising association concerned with the advertising agency business; and Marketing Science Institute, a research organization dedicated primarily to activity that will contribute to the emergence of a science of marketing and to

---

EXHIBIT 17

Sales and Marketing Executives-International
Executive Development Program

DURATION: 4 weeks (2 weeks for 2 consecutive years).
PARTICIPANTS: Upper middle- and top-level executives.
GROUP SIZE: 400.
AIM: To help the executive renew his enthusiasm to stimulate
    fresh thinking; improve his skills for managing; add to his
    knowledge for broader perspective; open resources for
    profitable volume; and increase confidence in problem
    solving.
PROGRAM: *First year*—Improvement of Executive Effectiveness;
    Improving Management of the Sales Force; Planning and
    Controlling the Marketing Effort; Current Marketing
    Problems I; Marketing Simulation. *Second year*—The
    Management Process; Marketing Decision Making; Market-
    ing Management; Current Marketing Problems II; Mar-
    keting Simulation.
TEACHING METHODS: Lecture, discussion, case, role playing.

---

the increased application of scientific techniques to the understanding and solving of marketing problems.

All these professional associations are striving to assist their
members in the attainment of greater skills and knowledge in
the field of marketing; their impact, in terms of the number of
individuals they can reach, is limited. The role of the professional associations, therefore, most likely will continue to be
important but somewhat less so than that of the individual, the
company, or the college and university.

Guidelines for the
Future

The marketing executive of the future must be equipped to manage change of all kinds—both internal and external, domestic and international. The most important changes in marketing will occur from forces at work in our society—economic, governmental, social, and technological. These forces have, and will continue to have, a profound impact on business and on the work and responsibilities of managers in marketing. Also of significance will be trends toward automation, international business activity, business-government relations, and technological advances from scientific and industrial research.

MANNING THE NEW FRONTIERS

The future qualifications of marketing executives will differ from current qualifications. The differences will result from a change in the emphasis of the top management function from finance to marketing, a change in the number of marketing managers needed in the future, the need for a knowledge of international marketing, and an increase in the number of marketing tools available—which will amplify the need for new knowledge to use and apply these tools.

To meet the demands of change in the years ahead, marketing executives will require new skills and additional knowledge in each of the following areas: creativity, entrepreneurship, behavioral sciences, marketing planning, international marketing, customer orientation in depth, information management, quantitative methods, systems analysis and control, and computer applications.

WEAKNESSES IN CURRENT DEVELOPMENT PLANNING

The emerging trends and their implications for managers in marketing point to the importance of marketing skills and knowledge. Yet the majority of management development programs in all areas—business and industry, colleges and universities, professional associations—give insufficient emphasis to marketing. The deficiencies may be summed up as follows:

1. Most companies have marketing executive development programs that are inadequate to meet the demands that continuing and accelerating change will present in the years ahead. Lacking is a scientific approach to one of the most important problems currently faced by top management—the development of managerial personnel, especially in marketing. Few companies have programs aimed at solving this problem.

2. The executive development programs offered by most colleges and universities place too little emphasis on marketing. In the light of current trends, marketing deserves more than secondary importance in the university executive development programs.

3. The scarcity of outstanding professional association programs—and the wide variation among the programs themselves—appears to call for improvement in this area if marketing executives are to be prepared to meet the challenges of the future.

Certain changes all along the line are vital if marketing executives are to be successfully trained for the job that lies ahead.

RECOMMENDATIONS FOR COMPANIES

Establish formal programs. As more and more companies adopt the customer-oriented marketing concept, formal marketing executive manpower planning and development programs should be established. With such programs, companies will develop qualified marketing staffs which are needed to implement new marketing programs.

State program philosophy and goal. Companies should make every effort to state explicitly the philosophy and objective of any marketing executive development program. In this way direction can be given to the program and the results measured.

Sponsor and support managerial development. Top management must establish sponsorship and support of marketing executive development. Only then will the climate and responsibility for developing marketing executives be set throughout the organization.

Evaluate programs. Companies should establish formal methods to evaluate the effectiveness of marketing executive development programs. Considering the huge sums of money being spent by industry for executive development and the little that is being done in evaluating the effectiveness of these programs, it is clear that one of the voids to be filled by corporations lies in the establishment of a formal method to evaluate the effectiveness of marketing executive development programs. To measure the effectiveness of these programs, however, the objectives must be clearly defined.

Develop more specialists. Business seems to be seeking marketing generalists. Many university executive development programs are aimed at developing generalists. Business must provide more programs and training activities necessary to develop the many marketing specialists who will still be needed. There appears to be a current imbalance in the development of marketing generalists and marketing specialists.

Increase use of seminars and programmed learning. Companies must increase the number of corporate and noncorporate seminars in marketing management, computer applications, creativity, systems analysis and control, international marketing, and other knowledge areas as the company needs demand. The application of programmed learning in marketing should be employed wherever feasible and practicable.

Improve recruitment and selection techniques. Corporations must develop a sophisticated selection process to find well-educated potential marketing managerial talent. Because the problems, organization, and policies of each company differ, the needs of each company for marketing executives also will be somewhat different. Consequently, each marketing executive development program will be somewhat different. On-the-job rotation assignments under competent supervision will undoubtedly provide the particular experiences needed to meet each company's idiosyncrasies. For this purpose, on-the-job assignments may prove to be the best method to develop marketing executives to meet the challenges of the future.

On the other hand, exposure, practice, and rotation on the job may not be enough. The information revolution will require marketing executives to be fed facts faster through electronic data processing. Data concerning marketing trends must reach managers as speedily as possible so that they have an opportunity to interpret and act upon them. They must learn how to apply and manage this flood of information in decision making.

Explain needs to educators. To explain their marketing

108

needs more completely and persuasively, corporations must make a determined effort to bring college and university educators to corporate headquarters. Many students are currently being graduated from college and university campuses throughout this nation with majors in the sciences, for example, but without the slightest idea of the complexities of the marketing function in business. Yet corporations will need executives with a greater degree of sophistication, especially in marketing, to meet the challenges of the years ahead. If colleges and universities will determine business needs and wants in terms of skills and qualifications for marketing executives, they can more accurately plan programs to satisfy these needs. And educators will be in a better position to explain the subject of marketing to their students.

RECOMMENDATIONS FOR COLLEGES AND UNIVERSITIES

Determine needs of business. Colleges and universities must determine the needs and wants of business on a continuing basis through carefully planned and supervised research. It is evident that corporations will always need marketing specialists —yet they like these men to have a broad business background. These same companies, nevertheless, generally recruit candidates who have had courses in the various marketing specialities. There appears to be a paradox here.

Develop programs to fill needs. Once the training needs are determined, colleges and universities should develop more specialized programs geared to meet them. The need for specialists might be recognized by the offering of additional courses, over and above the master's degree, in the marketing specialty. For higher levels of marketing management, colleges might find it advisable to offer a degree somewhere between a Master of Business Administration and a Doctor of Philosophy. Perhaps the degree might be a Professional in Business Administration.

Cooperate with business and industry. Institutions of higher

109

learning must establish and maintain effective cooperation with industry. This cooperation could exist in a wide variety of ways, including a continuous effort to talk over problems, an extension of the use of sabbaticals so that managers may continue to learn at the university and faculty may continue to learn in the firm, and a provision for more cooperative training programs that allow students to gain practical work experience in industry.

Define objectives and philosophies. Colleges and universities should clearly spell out in writing their objectives and philosophies in the area of marketing. Few institutions have actually done this. And almost every college and university interprets its mission differently. Once the direction has been established, the way will be open for the establishment of programs that can better assist in developing marketing executives for the future. The programs then can be evaluated in terms of these objectives as well.

Publicize programs. Institutions of higher learning should publicize their executive development programs, with greater emphasis than in the past on marketing. These programs should concentrate mainly on teaching the knowledge and skills described in Chapter 2 as being required of future executives in marketing.

RECOMMENDATIONS FOR PROFESSIONAL ASSOCIATIONS

Disseminate findings. Professional associations should communicate the results of conferences and research studies on a more extensive basis, especially to colleges and universities.

Provide small-group sessions. At educational meetings, large group sessions should be broken down into smaller seminar groups to allow for cross-fertilization of ideas among members with similar interests.

Sponsor regional conferences. The associations, which publish a number of excellent research studies, should sponsor regional conferences where these studies can be used as texts for discussion groups.

Promote programs more effectively. Professional associations should more effectively publicize their programs—to corporations and institutions of higher learning. The associations should also investigate the possibility of lowering membership and conference costs so that companies might find it more profitable to join the association rather than to conduct special conferences and courses at the company each time a special need arises.

Conduct studies to determine marketing needs. Professional associations should conduct studies to determine more accurately the marketing executive development needs of business. Continual study and review also should be carried out to determine the methods to meet these needs.

Armed with this information, the associations would be in a unique position to propose and to communicate standards for the development of future marketing executives. This would benefit not only the associations but also the companies and the institutions of higher learning.

Conduct additional research in special areas. Research should be conducted for the following purposes:

- To determine valid and reliable selection criteria for marketing executives. More accurate criteria are needed to assess an individual's potential in marketing.
- To determine the applicability of new quantitative and research tools to the field of marketing.
- To formulate a common terminology and understanding of marketing among corporations, institutions of higher learning, and professional associations.

PERSONAL ACTION

The practicing or potential marketing executive will face many challenges in the years ahead. He must train himself to fit all the many definitions which have been applied to the "manager of marketing." He must be a risk taker, a planner, a human relations specialist. He must be familiar with computer technology, sales planning, production scheduling, systems control, and other marketing tools; and he must possess imagination, ideas, creativity, and innovative skills.

Above all, the marketing manager must be a man of vision and adaptability. For, as change is the keystone of the market of tomorrow, so the ability to cope with change—and to profit from it—must be the keystone of the marketing executive of the future.

Bibliography

BOOKS

Alderson, Wroe, *Marketing Behavior and Executive Action,* Richard D. Irwin, Inc., Homewood, Ill., 1957.

Andrews, Kenneth R., *The Effectiveness of University Management Development Programs,* Division of Research, Harvard Business School, Boston, 1966.

Buell, Victor P., *Marketing Management in Action,* McGraw-Hill Book Company, 1966.

Dauten, Paul M., (ed.), *Current Issues and Emerging Concepts in Management,* Houghton Mifflin Company, Boston, 1962.

Davis, Robert T., *Performance and Development of Field Sales Managers,* Division of Research, Harvard Business School, Boston, 1957.

Drucker, Peter F., *The Practice of Management,* Harper and Row, New York, 1954.

Gordon, Robert A., and James E. Howell, *Higher Education for Business,* Columbia University Press, New York, 1959.

Howard, J. A., *Marketing: Executive and Buyer Behavior,* Columbia University Press, New York, 1963.

Houston, George C., *Manager Development—Principles and Perspectives,* Richard D. Irwin, Inc., Homewood, Ill., 1961.

Lazo, Hector, and Arnold Corbin, *Management in Marketing,* McGraw-Hill Book Company, Inc., New York, 1961.

Mahoney, Thomas A., *Building the Executive Team: A Guide to Management Development,* Prentice-Hall, Inc., Englewood Cliffs, N.J., 1961.

Merrill, Harwood F., and Elizabeth Marting (eds.), *Developing Executive Skills,* American Management Association, Inc., New York, 1958.

Mitchell, Don G., *The Challenges Facing Management,* New York University Press, New York, 1963.

Oxenfeldt, Alfred R., *Executive Action in Marketing,* Wadsworth Publishing Company, Inc., Belmont, Calif., 1966.

Pegram, Roger M., and Earl L. Bailey, "Manpower Crisis," in *The Marketing Executive Looks Ahead,* National Industrial Conference Board, New York, 1967.

Pierson, Frank C., *et al., The Education of American Businessmen,* McGraw-Hill Book Company, New York, 1959.

Towle, Joseph W. (ed.), *Ethics and Standards in American Business,* Houghton Mifflin Company, Boston, 1964.

Yoder, Dale, H. G. Heneman, John C. Turnbull, and C. Harold Stone, *Handbook of Personnel Management and Labor Relations,* McGraw-Hill Book Company, New York, 1958.

PERIODICALS

Adams, Velma, "How to Avoid a Manpower Crisis," *Business Management,* May 1967.

Ansoff, H. I., "The Firm of the Future," *Harvard Business Review,* September–October 1965.

Bienvenu, Bernard J., "Is Business Developing the Right Kind of Manager?" *Personnel,* May–June 1964.

Britt, Steuart Henderson, "The Obsolescent Marketing Man," *Sales Management,* August 3, 1962.

———, "How to Identify the Marketing Men You'll Need Tomorrow," *Business Management,* May 1967.

"Businessman of the Future," *Nation's Business,* January 1964.

"Business School with a Rising Star," *Business Week,* May 2, 1964.

"Computers Begin to Solve the Marketing Puzzle," *Business Week,* April 17, 1965.

Cyert, Richard M., and William R. Dill, "The Future of Business Education," *Journal of Business,* July 1964.

DePasse, Alfred B., and George P. Butler, "Grow Your Own Marketing Talent," *Nation's Business,* September 1959.

Ferguson, Laurence L., "Better Management of Managers' Careers," *Harvard Business Review,* March–April 1966.

"Getting More Out of the Graduate," *Business Week,* June 18, 1966.

Healy, James H., "Six Challenges for Tomorrow's Manager," *Dun's Review and Modern Industry,* October 1964.

House, Robert J., "Management Development Is a Game," *Harvard Business Review,* July–August 1963.

Keener, J. W., "Marketing's Job for the 1960's," *Journal of Marketing,* January 1960.

Kuriloff, Arthur H., "An Experiment in Management—Putting Theory Y to the Test," *Personnel,* November–December 1963.

Lazo, Hector, "Marketing Manager: Who the New Executive Is and What He Will Do," *Printers' Ink,* January 3, 1958.

Levinson, Harry, "A Psychologist Looks at Executive Development," *Harvard Business Review,* September–October 1962.

May, W. F., "Management in the Coming Decade," *Vital Speeches,* February 15, 1965.

"New Realities Facing Management," *Iron Age,* January 6, 1966.

Rathbone, M. J., "What Kind of Managers for Tomorrow's World?" *Vital Speeches,* April 1, 1965.

St. Thomas, Charles E., "A Basic Guide to Marketing for the Smaller Company," *Industrial Marketing,* June 1959.

Schuler, S., "How to Keep From Going Out of Style; Executive's Problems of Job Obsolescence," *Nation's Business,* February 1965.

Spencer, John A., "Tomorrow's Demands for Marketing Talent," *Sales Management,* July 21, 1961.

Stull, Richard Allen, "Management Challenges for the 1970's," *Advanced Management Journal,* January 1965.

"The AMA and Its Objectives," *Journal of Marketing,* October 1963.

"The Marketing Executive: Industry's New Crown Prince," *News Front,* August 1963.

"Tomorrow's Executive: New Dimensions You'll Need," *Nation's Business,* February 1965.

"Top Flight Marketing Needed," *Iron Age,* September 27, 1963.

Vetter, Eric W., "The Nature of Long Range Manpower Planning," *Management of Personnel Quarterly,* Summer 1964.

Wagner, D., "Educating Future Managers," *Administrative Management,* September 1965.

MISCELLANEOUS

Bond, Floyd A., Dick A. Leabo, and Alfred W. Swinyard, *Preparation for Business Leadership—Views of Top Executives,* Michigan Business Reports No. 43, Bureau of Business Research, Graduate School of Business Administration, University of Michigan, Ann Arbor, 1964.

Luck, David J., *Marketing Education in the United States,* Marketing Science Institute, Philadelphia, 1964.

Report on ANA's Advertising Management Development Program, prepared by Herbert Ahlgren, Association of National Advertisers, New York, July 23, 1962.

Index

Index

About the Author

Patrick J. Montana is Assistant Dean of the Graduate School of Business Administration at New York University. He holds degrees from Long Island and New York universities.

Prior to assuming his present position, Dr. Montana served as Associate Professor of Marketing and Consultant, Executive Development Programs, at Drexel Institute of Technology. He was also affiliated with Long Island University as Assistant Dean of the College of Business Administration, Chairman of the Management Department, and Associate Professor of Marketing and Management.

Dr. Montana is the author of a number of articles that have appeared in national publications and has lectured at the IBM Management School, New York University's Graduate School of Business Administration, and the Congress for International Progress in Management. In addition, he has done consulting work for various industrial corporations. Dr. Montana is a member of the American Marketing Association, American Society for Training and Development, American Management Association, and New York Personnel Management Association.